Praying is (Not) Hard

Other books by Erica

Holy Doubt
The Holy Doubt Journal

PRAYING

IS

(NOT)

HARD

Finally Let Go of the Baggage That
Keeps You From Talking with God

ERICA BARTHALOW

For you, dear reader,
that you may find joy in talking with
your Father, and that praying
will become as natural as
your next breath.

Contents

"The one concern of the devil is to keep Christians from praying. He fears nothing from prayerless studies, prayerless work, and prayerless religion. He laughs at our toil, mocks at our wisdom, but trembles when we pray."

– SAMUEL CHADWICK

It's time to make the devil tremble.

CHAPTER ONE

It's Complicated

One hundred twenty, one hundred twenty-one . . . Sunlight streamed through the stained glass windows of my childhood church as I silently counted each golden rectangle. My ears perked up as I heard the guest speaker for the morning, a missionary, drop the bomb that would set the stage for an epic struggle. Casually dropping the words as if they were as natural and normal as brushing his teeth, he said, "After my morning prayer time, which usually lasts a couple of hours . . ."

Wait. What?

Cue the scratching record. Did he just say he usually prays for a couple of hours? Every day? I remember scanning the room, my head on a swivel like a barn owl searching for a mouse, trying to read the faces of the people around me to see if they too were shocked and discouraged by this man's comment. Seeing no such visible signs of distress, I remember thinking, *Well, I must be a huge failure. The lone weirdo. The only one who struggles in this area.*

At that point in my life, I was lucky to pray for a couple of minutes. And certainly not every day. In fact, as I recalled my last prayer time, I seemed to remember my head lolling to one side, my eyelids drooping, and my mind wandering off right before I dropped into a light slumber.

My brain raced down a dark hole of self-condemnation. *What was wrong with me? Why didn't I pray for hours every day? What would my life be like if I did? Why was this prayer thing so hard? I mean, I knew how to talk for goodness' sake.* On and on those questions marched through my mind like the drum major at a homecoming game.

I found myself wondering if everyone was lying when they claimed to enjoy praying. Why wasn't that my story? For me, prayer was a dry, dull experience. Something I *had* to do instead of something I looked forward to.

But I left church that day wanting to do better. No, *vowing* to do better. Tomorrow morning would be the first day of my brand new powerful prayer routine. I could already picture it in my mind. Rising before dawn, I would pour myself a cup of milk (I didn't drink coffee back then, for shame), and I would spread my Bible on the bed in front of me and read and pray for an hour. The plan was set. My resolve, strong.

Five-thirty came early the next morning. I've never understood that statement actually, because by its very nature it comes at the same time twice a day, so it can't be early. But I digress. Can you guess what happened? Did I pop right out of bed, awake and alert, ready to read my Bible and pray? Nope. Not even close. Instead, as I stared at the alarm clock with bleary, sleep-crusted eyes, it was as if my finger contained a magnet that was drawn to the snooze button. I reached over and hit it so many times I barely had time to run out the door and make it to school before the tardy bell rang.

Another failure. If I were writing my yearbook superlative, I would have labeled myself: least likely to succeed in prayer. *Why couldn't I get it together?*

And there I was stuck, like those piano keys or computer keys that refuse to budge no matter how much you bang on them. Not for a couple of months, or even a couple of years, but a couple of decades. Stuck in a continual cycle of wanting to pray, vowing to pray, making a plan to pray, and then . . . not praying.

Maybe you can relate? Perhaps you too look around on Sunday mornings and secretly wonder, *Am I the only one who struggles with prayer?* Or maybe you just think, *Why is this so darn hard?!* Perhaps you've felt frustrated that you can't seem to pray for more than a few minutes. You really want to, but it just never seems to happen. Or maybe there's something you just can't quite put your finger on that keeps you from really enjoying your time in prayer—when you can find the time.

Maybe you feel silly, or even a little ashamed, that you haven't developed a regular, life-giving habit of prayer. Perhaps you wonder if you're doomed to a lackluster or nonexistent prayer life because you just can't sit still and focus. You have a deep desire to spend time in God's presence, but when you finally sit down to do it . . . Where was I? Oh yes, your mind wanders, or you walk away feeling disappointed or let down. Maybe with yourself, or sometimes even with God. And worse, you've lost hope that anything will ever change. You've accepted that prayer will always be a struggle. I know those feelings all too well.

The Resistance

When I first felt a stirring to write about prayer, I assumed I'd eaten some bad chicken (salmonella—the harbinger of crazy thoughts), and I immediately proceeded to resist the idea like a toddler with a Texas-sized knot in her hair fights a hairbrush. I told God, "Uh-uh! You've got the wrong girl. Are you confused? I'm no expert on prayer!" (Like he didn't already know that!)

Every time the thought popped into my head I protested it with gusto and tried (quite successfully, mind you) to come up with a list of all the reasons why I wasn't qualified and should not, in fact, even attempt to write about prayer. What did I possibly have to offer to a conversation on the subject? However, I just couldn't seem to escape the thought. It nagged at me, eventually becoming harder to shake than a summer cold. And when I finally calmed down just a little bit, I sensed God say, "Exactly."

Huh? What did that even mean?

You see, I've read books from the prayer experts and been inspired but slightly disappointed and disheartened because no matter how hard I tried, I just never could relate or seem to achieve their level of excitement and joy about prayer. I wanted that to be my story so desperately, and yet I couldn't figure out how to bridge the gap between what I knew in my head and what I wanted to do and what I actually did. No amount of wishing or good intentions seemed to help.

Until one day I finally realized (actually, I'm quite sure it was God's great mercy and kindness) it wasn't my desire to pray that was broken. It was some sneaky saboteurs that were constantly stalling my progress. That realization changed everything and set me on an entirely new path. And I believe it can do the same for you!

There's a place for experts–the Lord knows I need them! But I'm the girl to walk with you on this journey not because I'm an expert on prayer, but because I'm an expert in the struggle. I wasn't supposed to write a book about prayer. I was supposed to write about all the ways we get distracted and derailed from actually praying. That I can do. Believe me, I can do that! Because my friend, I've got issues. But God had a plan to help me work through them, and if you too struggle with some of these same issues, you're in the right place because he wants to help you too!

For the Love

I'm a runner. But I'm not a running evangelist. Well, I did try to convert my husband into a runner many moons ago, but that's another story for another day. I run because I like the way I feel–after I've done it. Because I don't actually love the act itself, it's easy for me to let it slip. Before I know it six months have passed and I've lost all progress. My muffin top is rolling over the band of my running shorts, and my thighs are rubbing together like a Boy Scout trying to start a fire with two sticks.

But, pilates. That's a completely different story. I do pilates because I love it. I love the way I feel while I'm doing it *and* after I've done it. Perhaps right now praying for you is like running for me. You have to force yourself to do it, and because it's such a struggle, it's easy to let it slip. Before you know it, a month has gone by and you haven't prayed at all. I get it. I've been there for more years than I'd like to admit, but I'm believing that by the end of this book, praying will be for you like pilates is for me. You'll enjoy the act itself as well as all of the benefits. I'm proof that this *can* happen. It can be your story too–no actual exercising required!

But as we know oh so well, it won't just happen. We need a plan to get there. And that's exactly what this book is: a plan and a guide. To help us recognize and dismantle the roadblocks and hang-ups that are keeping us from God. These are real issues that we can deal with. God is not hiding from us, and we're not just bad at praying. Sometimes it's the stuff inside our own heads that holds us back. Together, we'll unpack it and you'll make small, but significant, progress with each chapter. Pinky promise.

Following each chapter there's an invitation to practice praying, spending a few moments in the presence of God, asking him to reveal how the words of the chapter relate to your life. Please don't skip this part. We start really small (More on this later. Spoiler alert: it's really good.), but these moments spent actually talking to God are where the real change happens. You can do it! Decide right now you're going to do the work to finally break through.

Jesus wants prayer to be so much more than something we check off our to-do list for the day. He wants to write new chapters of joy over our chapters of discouragement and frustration. He wants to turn prayer from a struggle into a strength. I know that might feel impossible right now. You may have even rolled your eyes a little bit when you read that sentence. Perhaps as you're reading these words, a small voice is whispering in your ear, "This is just who you are. You're not good at praying. Nothing will ever change. You should just give up now. Don't waste your time."

This book is going to help you quiet that voice and those lies. You *can* have a different story. And I truly believe the subtle changes you'll experience as you read through each chapter will add up to a big difference by the time you turn the final page. It did for me. Towards that end there are exercises at the end of each chapter that are designed to help you break through and finally lay down your baggage about prayer for good. Don't feel like you have to do every single exercise (though you definitely can). Just pick one that seems particularly applicable to you and go for it!

When God created you, he dreamt of the conversations the two of you would have. He holds the answers to your deepest questions and the solutions to your biggest problems. He longs to give you wisdom that's greater than you can imagine and satisfy the longings in your heart that were meant to be filled by him alone. Whether you've spent an hour, a day, a year, or a decade stuck inside your head and stuck in prayer, you don't have to stay there. If you're ready for a new story, let's get started.

A word about the prayer practice at the end of each chapter: Doctors and lawyers (both professions where it seems highly important that they get things right) are allowed to "practice" medicine and law, respectively. I think we should give ourselves permission to practice prayer. Deal? You can start with the words below and then add a few of your own. You can do it!

Let's pray together right now.

God, I really want to love talking to you.
Right now, I admit it's a struggle and I'm skeptical
that things will ever change. But I want it to.
Please open up my heart and my mind to receive
everything you have for me as I read these words.
Let the story I'm starting with today be different
from the one I end with.
Amen.

Breakthrough Exercises

1. Write down the reasons you think it's hard for you to pray. Every. Last. Reason. No reason is too small–or too big. There's something about seeing those things that have held you back written down in black and white. It's hard to deal with something if you haven't defined or recognized it. As you work your way through this book you'll begin to face those issues and find a path forward.

2. Have you resigned yourself to the fact that you're always going to struggle to pray? Do you believe you're just bad at prayer?

   The things we tell ourselves and allow our hearts to believe have a way of shaping us. If you have believed that you'll always struggle to pray, try replacing that thought today with this one: *I can actually enjoy talking with God.* It might seem funny, but repeat it to yourself until you believe it!

3. What do you think the benefits of prayer are? How can knowing these benefits help you make prayer a daily practice that you enjoy?

CHAPTER TWO

Unspoken

Under the slightly strobing fluorescent lights in my church youth room, we stood in a misshapen circle holding hands and sharing prayer requests. My youth group was the one place where I felt completely safe and understood, but that particular night, when it was my turn to share a need, I offered a soft, "unspoken," with a shrug of my shoulder and my eyes glued to the floor.

In case you're unfamiliar with this nineties trend practiced by youth groups across America, if you wanted prayer but didn't want to share the details you would just say, "unspoken." A few people would murmur a supportive "Umm-hmm," and then they would move on to the next request.

Here's what you need to know about this habit that has gone the way of tight-rolled jeans and various other unfortunate fads from my childhood. My unspoken prayer request was the thing I felt most deeply, and it was the most honest thing about me or someone that I loved. And I was afraid to speak it out loud, even among friends.

When I began this journey, trying to lay aside my baggage about prayer, this is where the Lord started. He took his finger and pointed right to the secret, unspoken things. The things I was afraid to say out loud because I thought it made me a bad Christian or less spiritual than someone else. He had to expose them because, for the most part, I wasn't even aware I was carrying them around at all. Maybe you're carrying a few of these unspoken things too? Sometimes they go unexamined for our entire lives and we just drag them around like golf clubs at the airport, clumsy, awkward, and inconvenient. But I believe the Lord wants to help us identify them and lay them down as we work our way through the pages of this book.

Life coaches have become extremely popular in recent years. These individuals go through countless hours of training to learn how to ask probing questions that will lead you to the right answers and solutions to your specific problem. A good life coach's goal isn't to give you answers but to ask the right questions that will lead *you* to the answer. Consider me your very own prayer life coach, because I'm about to ask you some pretty personal questions.

If you'll trust me for a minute, it's time for a little exercise that the Lord used to help expose some of my hidden feelings, and it may be helpful for you too. Don't worry, you don't have to break a sweat or rearrange the furniture in your living room. You can do this exercise in your mind. That's the kind of exercise I like.

Ready?

Tune out everything happening around you right now, and imagine you're standing in the most jaw-droppingly beautiful room you've ever seen, kind of like the Altar'd State dressing rooms. (If you've never been to this store and used their dressing rooms, you're missing out on a spiritual experience. I tell people that's what my closet is going to look like in heaven.) Massive cascading curtains billow on a soft breeze that carries the sweet scent of your favorite candle. At the center of it all is God, sitting on the most breathtaking throne covered in jewels sparkling and glinting in the light. It's like nothing you've ever seen or imagined. Got it? Can you see it in your mind?

As you're standing there in that room in front of God I want you to focus on his face. When his eyes meet yours, what do you see? As you stand there in his presence, what does his face look like? Actually picture it. I'll wait.

When I did this for the first time, God's face was indistinct, fuzzy. I couldn't see any details. Maybe you're having the same issue. But I want you to focus on his facial features. As he sees you standing in front of him, do his eyes crinkle and his lips break into a smile? Or does he look slightly annoyed and inconvenienced?

Now, imagine what his face looks like when he hears your voice. Do you picture him up there rolling his eyes and saying to Gabriel, "Ugh! It's this one again. I've got so much going on. I wish she'd just leave me alone!" Or do you catch him saying, "Look! It's my daughter! She's talking to me. She's choosing to spend time with me!" as he leans closer to hear what you have to say?

I hope you visualized the latter, but if I'm honest, when I first did this I pictured God slightly bothered and not at all overjoyed to see or hear from me. Cold realization spread through me like a punishing January wind. I had no idea I carried such a negative picture of how God felt about me in my heart and mind.

Portraits of God

Maybe you were surprised by what you saw too? Perhaps you grew up in a home where you were to be seen and not heard, and it's still hard for you to believe anyone is excited to hear from you, let alone God. Maybe it's really easy for you to believe that you're an annoyance and a bother. Perhaps you picture God like your earthly father, too busy with his own pursuits to be interested in yours.

Before we get much further, let's talk about this idea that we're bothering God when we pray. It's a common hang-up. In fact, you know you suffer from it when you start your prayers with, "God, I know this is a small thing, and you've got a lot of other really important things going on, but if you don't mind, I could really use your help . . ."

Where do you think this idea came from, that whatever we're talking to God about is small and insignificant to him? Who gave us the idea that God is too busy for us? Do you think it came from God? Or someone else? Perhaps even the enemy of our souls? I think it's the latter. God is not put out by your prayers; he loves to hear your voice. Repeat that whenever you catch yourself starting your prayers like an apology.

I'm going to say something here that may shock you to your very core. Are you ready? God is not like us. You're probably thinking, "Umm, that is not a shocker. At. All." Okay, you're right, it shouldn't be a shocker. Even though we know this in our heads, we can easily slip into thinking he *is* like us, just so we can wrap our brains around him. We don't have a category for his otherness. But the problem with thinking God reacts like us should be obvious, and here's how it applies to our current conversation. For God to be too busy, too preoccupied with other things to be bothered with our needs, it would mean his ability and capacity to do things is limited. But our God is limitless. He is the ultimate multitasker.

After that exercise, it became increasingly clear that my picture of how God views me wasn't at all in line with what the Bible says. Its pages are full of verses that essentially tell us to wear God out with our requests,[1] to pray about everything,[2] that he numbers the hairs on our heads,[3] and collects our tears[4]. That doesn't sound like someone who thinks we're a nuisance. That sounds like someone who is almost obsessive about us. In the best way possible, of course.

Slowly, I began to understand why God started with my distorted picture of him. Before we started exploring all the other hang-ups that were keeping me from praying, I needed to settle in my heart, once and for all, that God actually wanted to hear from me in the first place.

In order to resolve this, he invited me to the place where it all began. The place that gives us a glimpse of his original intent when it comes to how we would relate with him and why he created us.

I'm not sure I've read a Christian book recently that didn't include a reference to Adam and Eve–for good reason. In order to find healing we have to examine the moment where everything was broken. God invited me to a garden, and he's inviting you too. Let's listen in on an ancient conversation between God the Father, God the Son, and God the Holy Spirit.

> Then God said, "Let us make human beings in our image, to be like us . . . So God created human beings in his own image. In the image of God he created them; male and female he created them." (Gen. 1:26a-27 NLT)

Have you ever wondered why God created anything at all? Why would a God who neither needs, nor wants for anything, create the planet we live on–all the plants, birds, animals, and people? His words at the conclusion of each act of creation give us a clue. He said, "It is good." And on the final day he said the creation of man and woman was "*very good.*"

I believe he created all of it, and especially us, for his enjoyment. Not because he had to, but because he wanted to. There is a massive difference between doing something because you have to versus doing something because you want to. We were the crown jewel of his creation, created for his delight. God crafted Adam and Eve to enjoy his presence and for him to enjoy theirs.

God's original intent was for us to know only deep, in-person communion with him. How do I know this? Genesis tells us, "...the man and his wife heard the sound of the Lord God walking in the garden at the time of the evening breeze."[5] They recognized the *sound* of the Lord walking. Can you imagine? If you've ever moved into a new house, you know it takes a little while to get used to all the creaks and cracks of the floors and pipes so you're not reaching for a baseball bat every time you hear a noise. The fact that they recognized the sound of him coming meant it happened a lot. They'd been conditioned over time to recognize the sound. It was a regular occurrence. This means he must have approached often to be with them, speak to them, spend time with them. Perhaps they had a regular meeting time and spot. That was his original plan: to talk with us, to be with us. And it's still his plan. He wants the sound of our prayers to be as familiar and common to his ears as his presence was to Adam and Eve in the Garden of Eden.

But sin.

It warps and frustrates even the purest design. That's why God had to send Jesus to die for our sins so that we could once again experience that sweet friendship. But before sin entered the picture and marred everything, Adam and Eve walked in the perfection that God created and talked with him. Regularly.

Sinners in the Hands of an Angry God?

I have a strange confession to make: the book of Isaiah in the Bible is my absolute favorite. Most of the time when I tell people this they look at me like I have two heads or six eyes. I feel like there are two types of people in the world: those who love Isaiah, and those who absolutely hate it. There is no middle ground. I'm not sure what else it says about me that it's my favorite, but I think it's fair to say that I'm comfortable with (or at least accept) the idea of an angry, justice-doling God. And to be fair, Isaiah contains some of the most beautiful pictures of God's pursuit of humanity as well. It's a nuanced book to be sure. I think that's why I love it so much.

Before we can move on to our first hang-up, we need to return once again to our original picture of God. Let's go to his throne room again in our minds. Are you there? When you pictured God in your head, was he angry?

When my son was eight I got my very first ever brand-new car. No one else had ever owned this beautiful hunk of metal. My eyes had never before beheld such small numbers on an odometer. I may have been more in love with that Honda than what was proper.

Not even a couple days after we brought it home, I was sitting in the living room when the door to the garage swung open and my son burst in with hot tears running down his very red face. "Moooommmm," he bellowed through his hiccups and sniffles. "I s-s-scratched y-your caaar." Did I immediately jump up to console the kid? Ummm, no. I ran out to the garage to survey the damage. Sure enough. There was a long silver scratch down the driver's side door.

Why am I reliving and sharing such a traumatizing memory? Because if you pictured God angry when he looks at you, it's understandable that you might not choose to spend a lot of time in his presence. You might even be tempted to hide, or avoid him altogether. I know I've been there. More times than I'd care to admit.

There could be a ton of reasons why we might picture him angry. It might be because we've sinned or messed up in some way. But you know what? Even when we sin and mess up, he's still happy to hear our voice. Even, and maybe especially, when we screw up. I'm always proudest of my kids when they come to fess up.

After my initial panic and need to see how bad the car looked, I was so proud that Jacob came and told me what happened instead of trying to cover it up (which would have been a very useless endeavor). I have a sneaking suspicion that God is even more pleased when we choose to go to him and we fight the urge to hide, because hiding only halts our healing and holds up our wholeness.

Ultimately, our picture of God shapes our entire perspective on prayer. This one idea is so foundational for the rest of the conversations in this book that we have to spend enough time here to make sure we get this right. Do you know in your head that God loves you and delights in you but struggle to truly believe it? Do you have an easier time believing that God's attention and affection are meant for someone other than you?

As a kid who grew up in church, I remember singing *Jesus Loves Me* in rooms filled with flannel boards covered with paper cutouts of Bible characters and small primary colored chairs. Looking around the room, I'd sing the words, but I didn't really believe them. Those words conveyed a truth that was meant for others, not for me. I may as well have been singing, "Yes, Jesus loves you. Yes, Jesus loves you." I believed that. I could sing that with sincerity. To this day, I still have to work at accepting and believing that Jesus really loves *me,* and because of that love wants to hear my voice and talk with me.

Perhaps you too are realizing that you struggle to believe that God's love and his Word is for you. Maybe this chapter has made you aware that you carry a distorted picture of him in your head. Now is your moment. If God has been revealing some secret, unspoken attitudes and beliefs that are holding you back, now is the time to let them go. He not only wants to expose any warped views of him that you may have, he wants to redeem them and replace them with the truth.

I think now is a very good time to pray, because God is the only one who can set us free and give us an accurate picture of how he truly sees us.

God, search my heart today. Expose any hidden,
unspoken things that are keeping me from
connecting with you. If I have a warped picture
of you, please replace it with your truth.
Help me accept and believe in your love for me.
I know I can't do this on my own. I want to be free
of the feeling that I'm bothering you or that
you're annoyed when I come to you.
Reshape my perspective on prayer to reflect
what you long for it to be.
Amen.

Breakthrough Exercises

1. As humans we may not be great at multitasking, but God is not like us. If you struggle with the idea that God is bothered by your prayers, or he is too busy to listen, start to notice how often you have those thoughts. Notice when you begin your prayers like an apology. Practice approaching God with confidence.

2. Do you struggle to believe biblical promises and God's love is meant for you? Spend a little time right now exploring that and writing down any reasons why you might have bought into those lies.

3. Failure–the dreaded "F" word. It's actually taught you more than you realize. If you feel like a failure at prayer right now, what can you learn from that feeling? Chances are it's showing you some things that haven't worked, but how can you use that information to develop some practices that *do* work?

PART ONE

The Hang-Ups

CHAPTER THREE

Perfect

*"When it comes to prayer, God isn't grading essays;
he's talking to children."*

– TYLER STATON

When I was in second grade, the unthinkable happened. My music teacher at Berryton Elementary gave me a solo in our vocal music concert. *Me! A solo.* I remember belting out the words to *My Computer and Me* (it was as good as it sounds) daily in the front seat of my mom's car. In my mind and memories, I was amazing.

For weeks I practiced and visualized myself standing in front of my parents, grandparents, and all of my classmates while they thought to themselves, *What a nice voice she has. So lovely. She might be the next Mariah Carey.*

On the afternoon of the performance, as my classmates and I clumped together outside of the music room, a prickly, paralyzing fear swept over me. Digging my heels into the shiny hallway tiles like a stubborn goat, I refused to walk into the room. Various family members came out to the hallway trying to convince me it would be okay and that I should just go in and sing. Arguments about wasted hard work and long hours practicing were unsuccessful. I would not be convinced.

In the days leading up to that fateful non-performance, all alone in my bedroom I could belt that song out like Whitney Houston. (I hope you're enjoying all the references to the musical geniuses of my childhood.) But on the day of the musical, with an audience looking on, I was afraid I would mess up. So I didn't even try. It wasn't the first time, and it certainly wouldn't be the last, that I froze, immobilized by the idea that I wouldn't get something right, that I wouldn't be perfect.

The Pressure Cooker

Fast forward a few years. Lou Ellen and Etta were my heroes. I watched them show up faithfully, month after month, year after year, to pray together in a small overflow room off of our church sanctuary. In my mind, these ladies had prayer figured out. They were the world's greatest pray-ers. (Is that even a word? I don't think so. But we're going with it.)

The fact that they got in their cars and drove to the church to regularly meet with someone else in order to pray showed a commitment level that I envied–even if I wasn't quite sure I was ready to emulate it. I was doing good to *want* to pray. Alone. Silently. I had zero desire to pray out loud in front of other people. Ever. (We'll get to that in a minute.)

For now, let's start here. What does a perfect pray-er look like to you? Does a real-life person pop into your head? What do they do? What do they not do? Actually stop, take out a piece of paper and make a list that defines your idea of a perfect pray-er. Be as specific and thorough as you can. Don't worry about whether something is "right" or "wrong." Just write it down. This little exercise will help you figure out what your brain defines as "success" when it comes to prayer. For me, it was Lou Ellen and Etta. Faithful. Hungry. Bold. Maybe for you it's someone who:

- Prays for 30 minutes every day–or an hour
- Always has the right words
- Never makes excuses
- Is the first person people go to for prayer
- Never gets distracted

It could be a hundred different things, but this is a great place to begin because I'm guessing you've never taken the time to figure out what winning in prayer actually looks like to you. This was one of the most helpful things I ever did, and I'm guessing it will be helpful (and eye-opening) for you too.

Let's look again at the list above and your own personal list. Did you notice some of the words on it? Always. Never. Those are extreme words, full of so much pressure. I don't know about you, but whenever I feel pressured I immediately resist whatever activity is causing that feeling. Some people think, "Pressure! Bring it on! I eat pressure for breakfast!" while flexing in front of their bathroom mirror. That is not me. At. All. If I think I'm not going to do well at something I usually avoid doing it altogether.

This was certainly the case when it came to praying.

After completing the exercise above, I became increasingly aware that I felt pressure about so many things related to talking with God. Drilling down on the feeling, I discovered it all bubbled up from a need to be perfect–or to be perceived as perfect. By God and by other people. I felt pressure to not say anything wrong, to pray at the right time in the right way, and pressure to say everything so beautifully and eloquently that other people would be impressed when they heard me pray. So. Much. Pressure. I love this quote from Ruth Chou Simons, because I relate to it so much. She said, "Isn't it just like the enemy to derail us from the prize of knowing Jesus with the mirage of 'doing it right?'"[1] I just wanted to do it right. Whatever that means.

But perfectionism is a thief. Of all the things it steals from us, and it steals a lot, one of the biggest is our prayers. It's the first issue we're addressing because, of all the hang-ups we'll discuss, it's the one that keeps us from praying at all. Locked inside of our own heads, frozen by our fears and insecurities, the words just stay bottled inside. Never to be released. Because we'll never get them perfect. But as Winston Churchill said, "Perfection is the enemy of progress."[2] And we are all about progress on this journey towards talking with God.

As I perused my perfect pray-er list, I realized there were a couple of areas in particular where I felt I needed to be perfect or could achieve some sort of super pray-er status. When I held those ideas up to the light of day, I discovered some of them weren't very helpful and might not even be biblical.

Writing these ideas that I'd collected about prayer down on paper was the critical first step that helped me sort out what expectations about prayer were from God and what had been manufactured by me. It was the first step toward setting me free from the perfectionism that was sucking the life out of something that was meant to be life-giving. Which begs the question, where do our ideas about prayer come from anyway?

Early to Rise

For as long as I can remember, most of the teaching I heard about prayer centered around "giving the Lord the first part of your day," which I interpreted as, "get out of bed, lazy-bones." I know exactly where the idea came from, and the heart of it is good and biblical. Offering God our best and first is a principle found throughout Scripture.

The idea of getting up early to talk to God is mentioned often in the Psalms and a practice of Jesus himself. So it seems like a solid example to follow, but a rooster I am not. Nor have I ever been. So this particular emphasis on the early morning left me feeling like a failure every time a pastor or Sunday School teacher mentioned it. As I've already confessed, I have never been successful at getting up early–and staying awake–to pray. Maybe you can relate and you too have felt less than because you don't pray as soon as your eyes snap open for the day?

A quick Google search reveals a cascade of articles devoted to the beauty, and importance, of morning prayer. They don't come right out and say that it's the "correct" time to pray, but it's definitely implied. This left me wondering, *Is there one perfect time of day to pray? Am I a failure because I don't pray before I do anything else in the morning? Was I doomed to have my prayers fall on deaf ears because I prayed in the afternoon or evening?* These questions rattled around in my brain as I talked to the Lord on an early afternoon walk.

As my foot turned down a favorite path that would lead me over a well-worn wooden bridge with a picturesque view of the town where I live, I began to think about Jesus and all of the times he prayed in the Bible. I decided the best thing to do in order to find answers for these questions would be to open my Bible and make a list of what he actually did.

Here's what I found:

- He made a habit of prayer (Luke 5:16).
- He *did* pray in the morning (Mark 1:35).
- He prayed before doing some of his greatest miracles (raising Lazarus from the dead–John 11:41-42, walking on water–Matt. 14:23-27, feeding the five thousand–Matt. 14:19).
- He prayed when he was choosing his disciples (in other words, when he had a big decision–Luke 6:12).
- He prayed at night and *all* night (Luke 6:12).
- He prayed before eating (Matt. 26:27).
- He prayed when he was under stress (Luke 22:41-44).
- He prayed as he was dying (Luke 23:34, 46).

Basically, I discovered he prayed all the time. In any situation and every circumstance. Morning. Afternoon. Night. Whenever. Which reminds me of a verse penned by Paul in 1 Thessalonians 5:17, where he instructs us to, "Never stop praying." It's clear from looking at Jesus's life that he made talking to his Father a lifestyle not an event. Prayer was as simple as his next breath. His example proves that *any* time is a great time to talk to God. So where does all this pressure come from anyway?

Let's go back to our original question. Is it good to pray in the morning? Of course. Is it biblical to pray first thing when you get up? There are certainly Scriptures to back that up. But is it the only time God listens or wants to hear from you? Not even close.

Two words have become very helpful to me with this particular hang-up. Asking myself if a particular passage in Scripture is prescriptive or descriptive. In other words, is this showing me something I'm supposed to do, or is it describing something that was done? Did Jesus only pray in the morning? We can see that he did not. Did God listen more closely to his prayers in the morning? I don't think so.

So why did I feel this intense pressure to pray in the morning, or more accurately, why did I feel like I would earn more points with God if I did? All this pressure came from my ideas about what it meant to be a "good" Christian more than from our good God. Which leads us quite nicely to the next issue on my quest to be the "perfect" pray-er.

Odd and (Slightly) Irrational Fears

For most of my life, I've harbored a strange fear. I've been afraid of unwittingly becoming like the Pharisees in the Bible. Growing up in church, I was keenly aware that they were the religious people of their day. They thought they were oh-so-right, and then Jesus showed up and told them they were getting it all wrong. I did not want to be like them.

Jesus was so kind and compassionate to everyone in the New Testament–everyone except the Pharisees. He had no patience for their shenanigans. They took a good command from the Law of Moses, one that was meant to bring life and health, and added so many extra stipulations that the original intent of the law became warped, obscured, and impossible to follow. And Jesus wasn't having it.

It sent the fear of God rushing down my spine every time I read his words, "Woe to you, scribes and Pharisees, hypocrites! For you are like whitewashed tombs, which outwardly appear beautiful, but within are full of dead people's bones and all uncleanness. So you also outwardly appear righteous to others, but within you are full of hypocrisy and lawlessness."[3] Yikes! I definitely did not want Jesus to look at me and say, "You put on a good show, everyone thinks you're perfect, but your heart is a mess."

Reading about them I would often think, *how did they get like that?* Surely they didn't start out that way? I'm guessing their motives were pure at one point; all they wanted to do was please God and teach people how to follow him. But somewhere along the way they got sidetracked and the freedom found in following God was twisted into a rule-following show.

Now I certainly wasn't in full-on Pharisee mode. As you'll recall I didn't want to pray in front of people. That made my knees floppy, my heart race, and my armpits sweat. But in group prayer situations I spent more time critiquing and envying other people's prayers than I did focusing on God and entering his presence. I completely lost focus on what prayer is actually about, and I think that's the root of this hang-up. In trying to be perfect pray-ers, we make prayer all about us.

The Pharisees were probably some of the most eloquent, long-winded (more on this in chapter eleven) pray-ers of their time. I'm pretty sure they could stand on any street corner, or at the front of any synagogue, and blow you away with the power of their words. They were impressive. They were the "perfect" pray-ers of their day. But they weren't impressing God. He wasn't dazzled with their words because he could see what kind of heart those words were coming from–and it wasn't pretty. It was smelly, stinky, and dead.

Like the Pharisees, I've certainly been guilty of trying to impress people with my prayers. Which, by the way, never happens. Give me a paper and pen or keyboard and I can knock your socks off with words, but ask me to open my mouth and speak words out loud, and it's about to get real awkward. I've stood in prayer circles and been enamored (and intimidated) by the eloquent prayers of those around me. With each beautiful word uttered I've felt the pressure building in my soul. Pressure to say equally beautiful words when it was my turn to pray, and by the end of the prayer time I'd tied myself in knots and never truly connected with God at all.

As I brought this hang-up to the Lord, he gently reminded me that I was getting off track and suffocating under all this pressure because my focus was off. I was making prayer about me (or how awesome the people around me were at praying) rather than making it about him. I decided, in that moment, that I wanted to be a woman who is less concerned about perfection and more concerned about the pursuit of my Father.

But that sounds like a quote you might put on your desk or your wall, or "like" on social media and then promptly forget about the next time you're standing in a prayer circle feeling pressure to "perform" and say the perfect words. How do we actually live this noble ideal? How do we move it from a good idea in our minds to a reality that works its way into the fabric of our lives in a natural and unforced way?

We need to redefine what makes someone a perfect pray-er. We need to tear up or scratch through any ideas that are on our list that don't measure up to what God says makes him sit up and take notice. So what *does* impress God?

The Pressure is Off

Have you ever wondered what kind of prayer (or pray-er) truly pleases God? The prayers that bring him joy and delight? I think you might be surprised. You know who Jesus said impressed him? Children.

I love listening to the prayers of new believers and children. There's so much freedom in the way they talk with God. They don't censor themselves. There's nothing too small or silly, or too big and impossible to bring to him. I have a friend who was once feeling quite down about her wrinkles and the fact that all the wrinkle cream was so expensive, so she decided to talk to God about it. On her very next trip to Walmart there was a huge sale on her wrinkle cream. Nothing too small or silly, indeed. He listens and cares about it all. If it's important to you, it's important to God.

As my fingers hovered over the keyboard to write this chapter, I hesitated and procrastinated because I didn't want to edit. I want my words to be perfect–the first time. But that's not possible with writing. Believe me (and just about every other writer out there who's admitted it takes a ton of terrible words to get a couple of good ones). And it's not possible with prayer either. It's in the free flow of words that the best stuff comes out, and if you've ever listened to the prayers of children you know that's exactly how they pray. There is a complete and utter lack of self-consciousness. Whatever is on their mind, they say. And it's beautiful.

We've overcomplicated prayer so much that it's become a point of shame instead of a joy and the powerful weapon it was meant to be. So let's pause right here, right now, and just tell God what you're thinking about. He doesn't care if you offer him perfect words or first draft words. He doesn't care about edits; he delights in hearing your voice.

If you still need a little encouragement to get out of your own head and get the words flowing, join me at Ephesians 3:20. As I was reading this passage recently the words seemed to jump off the page. I love the way the Amplified Bible says it:

> Now to him who is able to [carry out his
> purpose and] do superabundantly more than all
> that we dare ask or think [infinitely beyond our
> greatest prayers, hopes, or dreams], according
> to his power that is at work within us . . .

Did you catch that? He is able to do *"superabundantly more"* than we can ever ask or even dream of asking. Kind of takes the pressure off, doesn't it? Suddenly it isn't about us having the right words, or remembering every request, and it becomes about God's ability to not only hear but to respond as only he can, in an over-the-top, extravagant way. "Superabundantly" means he is the God who takes our imperfect words and does immeasurably more. It means he takes our imperfect words and works his perfect plan.

We finally break free from the hang-up of perfectionism when we realize it's not about what we say, or how we say it, but who we say it to. When we recognize, "God is able to give more than we ask, and even more than we understand. Neither the narrowness of our knowledge nor the feebleness of our prayer will limit the richness of his gifts."[4] He is the God who takes our imperfect words and does more than we can ask, think, or imagine. That's always the goal with prayer: to get our eyes off of ourselves and onto God, helping us understand that nothing ever can–or ever will–limit him.

So the win, and the way to be "perfect" at prayer, is to just do it. That's it. Just pray. He's less concerned with the how, where, and why than we are. It's about the posture of our heart more than the words coming out of our mouth. He never asked or expected you to be perfect anyway.

But I get it. It might still be a struggle to just say those first imperfect words. If that's you, and you still feel stuck, try this simple prayer. Just say the name of Jesus. And if you're thinking, *Erica, that's not a prayer, it's a name,* I think you'll be interested to hear what Bob Goff says about it. He says, "Jesus isn't wowed by fancy words. Matter of fact, he said his name has all this kind of power. So what if we just [say] this . . . 'Jesus!' And if you're not impressed by this prayer, you haven't experienced the power of Jesus's name."[5]

I would echo Bob's words. As you say Jesus's name today, think about who he is. His might. His power. His goodness. His love and care for you. All of this and more, wrapped into one single word that changes us and changes everything–including our prayers.

Father, help me grasp the truth of Ephesians 3:20
today deep in my heart and in my head.
Help me understand that the strength and
effectiveness of my prayers don't rely on me, but on
you. Let me rest knowing that I don't have to have
beautiful or perfect words for you to hear me.
Set me free from the pressure to be perfect by helping
me focus on your perfection.
Amen.

Breakthrough Exercises

1. Identify a specific emotion you feel about prayer. It could be: indifference, hopelessness, frustration, anger, confusion, joy, etc. Now take a moment to present that emotion to God, unpacking all the reasons for this feeling and ask him to help you find some good emotions and experiences about prayer.

2. If you can, spend some time listening to a child pray. Let the simple openness and transparency of their prayers untangle some of your complicated feelings. Maybe even ask them to pray for you!

3. Spend some time reflecting on this chapter. Are there any areas of perfectionism holding your prayers back? Do you worry too much what other people think of your prayers? Do you worry that you just aren't eloquent enough? As you assess, take any issues that pop up to the Lord and ask him to help you let them go.

Hang-Up #2: Does it Really Matter?
Overcoming Monotony and Discouragement

CHAPTER FOUR

Breaking Bored

"Teach them to estimate the value of each prayer by
their success in producing the desired feeling; and
never let them suspect that how much success or
failure of that kind depends on whether they are well
or ill, fresh or tired, at the moment."

– C.S. LEWIS

When I was a kid I complained rather frequently about
being bored. What can I say? I was an only child with no
siblings to entertain (or annoy) me. My mom finally got
so exasperated that she said, "If you tell me you're bored
again, I'll give you something to do–and you won't like

it." Something about her tone communicated that she spoke the truth and I never complained about boredom to her again.

Maybe you've felt the affliction of this particular problem in your prayer life. I know I have. Much like the rest of my life, I'm a creature of habit, and my prayers frequently fall into the same old patterns and requests and even *I* get bored hearing my voice repeating the same problems, issues, and petitions over and over to God.

It's here that I readily acknowledge that the issue isn't with God, it's with me. God is not boring, but I'm human and I get bored–even in prayer. Acknowledging this fact, however, doesn't make the issue any easier to face. One thing I discovered on this journey toward being engaged and interested in prayer was that my unexamined thoughts (i.e. prayer is boring), patterns and habits were keeping me locked in my cycle of prayerlessness, and it became clear that if I wanted to make a change it was time to confront some of them. Nowhere was this more difficult and uncomfortable than the area around the emotions I feel about–and during–prayer.

The Value of Prayer

When I began to really dig down to the heart of this issue in my life I started by asking, *What exactly do I believe about prayer and the Bible?* Because the two are so very closely connected. We talked in a previous chapter about the things we believe about God, and while there is some overlap in the answer to this question, there is yet another layer I needed to pull back and examine.

Most of us would never say that prayer is unimportant or that we shouldn't do it (that's why you're reading this book!), but sometimes our actions can tell us more about what we truly believe than our words ever will. So can I ask you, *What do you honestly believe about prayer?* Your thoughtful answer to this question is the tipping point for a revolution in your prayer life. Once I grasped the power and connection with God that's available to us through prayer, I never approached it the same way again. But for years I just didn't get it.

When I started to get serious about dealing with my prayer issues, I felt like God dropped some questions into my mind (and if you know me well, you will not be surprised that God gets my attention with questions). Maybe they'll be helpful to you too as you uncover your true thoughts and feelings about prayer. See if any of these sound familiar to you:

1. After you've prayed for someone, do you catch yourself asking if there's something you can do?

2. Do you say you'll pray for someone and then never actually do it?
3. Are you surprised when God answers your prayers?
4. Do you roll your eyes (inwardly, of course) when people ask for prayer about "trivial" or "dumb" things?
5. How much time do you spend praying? Do you spend more time thinking about an issue or talking to friends about it than you spend talking to God about it?
6. When was the last time you sincerely asked someone to pray for you?
7. If God answered your prayers, would it make a real difference in the world?

Perhaps you can relate to one or two . . . or all seven? As it dawned on me that I did all of these things–Yes. All. Of. Them–I was stunned when I began to understand the underlying assumptions and beliefs that these questions revealed. If you answered yes to any (or all) of these questions you're not alone (ahem), but it may be a gentle warning that it's time for a little self-reflection.

Engaging in my own season of reflection, I realized that lurking behind my seemingly kind offer to do something for someone (please don't take this as an excuse to never perform an act of kindness for someone) immediately after I prayed for them was the belief that the prayer I had just prayed was insignificant. While it's wonderful to pair prayer with action, my words revealed that I subtly believed the prayer I'd just prayed wasn't doing anything.

Poking further, I noticed I would get irritated in group prayer situations when someone asked for prayer over something I deemed silly or inconsequential. Mulling over this attitude, I realized the people who asked for prayer over "dumb" stuff probably understood prayer far better than I did.

And don't get me started on asking for prayer. I *never* wanted to ask for prayer. Perhaps because I didn't want to be seen as needy, but more often, I realized that deep down I didn't think it would really make a difference. *What in the actual world?!* This is hard to admit as a person who has grown up in church and served in various ministry positions. And yet there it sat, staring me in the face, daring me to deny the truthfulness tucked tightly into the ugly revelation.

I started to understand that if I truly valued prayer and believed it worked, I would be clamoring– no, begging– for prayer *every* single time someone offered. I would seek people out to pray for me. Instead, whenever people asked for prayer requests in groups, I was the least likely person to pipe up. I don't think I'm alone in this either. I've found it's mostly crickets when I'm in group situations and someone asks for prayer requests.

Slowly, I began to see that I placed a very low value on prayer–and very little belief in the power of it. Of course it's going to be boring if I don't truly believe it matters or that God is actively listening and moving behind the scenes in response to my prayers. Once I began to understand the power and value of prayer it became far more exciting and I wanted to do it far more. But there were still some issues I needed to deal with to completely clear this hurdle of boredom.

In My Feelings

Nervously, I picked up my Bible and flipped to the burgundy satin ribbon that marked my last spot. As my fingers hovered over the thin paper I felt the familiar urge to just quit, give up. A persistent voice in the back of my head was asking, *What if you spend this time reading and it's just a big letdown? What if you don't feel anything? What if God doesn't speak to you? It would probably be better to just avoid it altogether rather than be disappointed. You've got a lot going on. You could just skip it today.*

Don't judge me, but I enjoy an emotional experience. I grew up in a Pentecostal church. I think that explains it all really. So I especially like having an emotional experience when I read my Bible and pray. While there's nothing inherently wrong with being passionate and feeling strong emotions about our time with God, it can go horribly wrong if our feelings become the focus. As C.S. Lewis so aptly points out in the quote at the beginning of this chapter, so much of what we feel (or don't feel) when we pray can be more readily attributed to our physical health and surroundings than the effectiveness of our prayers. Yet for so long I allowed my feelings to dictate when, how, or if I prayed.

No one wants to go through the motions like a robot without experiencing the presence of God, but there's also danger in exclusively chasing those feelings and labeling your prayer time good or bad based on how you feel in the moment. I became accustomed to using those feelings, tears, and emotional responses to validate the time I spent in prayer, to reassure me that it was worth the investment. If there were no tears or warm fuzzies you can guess how I felt about the practice.

The value of my prayer time was measured by how I felt while I was praying or after it was over. If there were no emotional feelings, it was boring. I was bored. And very likely to avoid it the next day. And the day after that. You see where we're headed, right? Now some of this was immaturity, but let's be honest, sometimes praying doesn't cause any emotional reactions or responses, and it's in those moments that we get to ask ourselves something: What's my motivation for prayer? Why do I do it? Why do I feel like I should? Is it because I believe it has power, someone told me that I should, Jesus did it, or some other reason altogether?

Perhaps you come from a tradition where you recited memorized prayers or read them from a book, and the idea of emotional or passionate feelings about Bible reading and prayer is a foreign concept to you. It's always been more of a ritual than something you felt deeply engaged with. I envy you a little bit, because as I've already admitted, for a long time my motivation to pray was to feel a certain way. To seek an emotional high. I went to God and my Bible to get a boost for my day or to find an answer for something I was dealing with.

While there's nothing wrong with any of this, it all has its place, it leads me very nicely to the main reason I got bored praying. My prayers (just like my Bible reading) was all about me. Sure, I sprinkled the occasional request for someone else in there, but most of the time it was about me. My needs, my desires, my dreams. Me, me, me, me, me. (At this point that old Toby Keith song *I Wanna Talk About Me* is on repeat in my brain–send help.)

When I started reading the Bible to learn what God was like instead of trying to find something that made me feel good or I could post on Instagram, I started to see a completely different path opening before me. One would think that reading the Bible and searching for how it affects you would be the most motivating way to read, but strangely it wasn't. When I began reading to learn about God, what he's like, how he responds and reacts, it became a feast of fresh discovery with every reading. There's always something new to learn about God. He's completely fascinating. And the more I learned about him, the more I wanted to learn.

I'd like to ask you another question now. (Shocking, I know. I am the question queen. My husband and kids love this about me.) Do you actually believe the Bible is true? Don't answer that right away, because I would have immediately shouted a resounding yes during this season of my life. But slowly, it became clear that I approached the Bible with a spirit of unbelief.

After reading verses like Romans 8:11 that said, " . . . the [same] Spirit that raised Christ from the dead lives in you . . ." I was dumbfounded. The words either seemed too amazing to be true and I downplayed or discredited them, or I made excuses about why I was somehow the lone exception excluded from the incredible promise expressed in this statement. Or sometimes I just didn't think about it all, rushing past the incredible power and absolutely ridiculous mercy and kindness of God that are contained in those words *and* available to me. Y'all! The Bible is scandalous! But so often I read it as if it was a book full of nice stories, stripping them of their power because I just didn't believe the wonder it spoke of was available to me. And I was oblivious to the fact that I did this. I had all the belief in the world in the power of God but doubted almost everything his Word said when it came to me.

For instance, take Philippians 4:6 which says, "Don't worry about anything; instead, pray about everything." It seemed like something I'd post on Instagram but doubt that God really meant it. Pray about *everything?* Worry about *nothing?* Yeah, right. I'll get right on that.

Perhaps, like me, you read something that seems too wonderful to be true (or too hard to put into practice) in the Bible and you immediately start downplaying it? Making excuses for God? Or thinking about how it applies to someone else, but not you? Or maybe you don't spend much time thinking about it at all?

Friend, if you're a believer, the Bible is full of promises for you–about you. Those precious words are not just for your super-holy neighbor or your pastor's wife. They are for Y-O-U. But if you have a hard time believing they apply to you, you're in good company. For years I was right there with you.

In case it seems like I'm talking out of both sides of my mouth here, because I said that I gained freedom when I stopped trying to make everything about me and turned my focus towards God, but in the very next breath I started talking about my spirit of unbelief, I promise it's not a contradiction at all. That attitude was making God small in my life (and my prayers). So confronting it was really less about me, and more about God.

So what does all this have to do with boredom, you might be wondering? I'm so glad you asked. When I started reading the Bible and believing it, applying it, and treating it like it wasn't just a nice book written for people in the past (or other people that I deemed more holy), my prayers came to life. I found boredom slipping further and further into my past and a brand new world of connection with God blooming in front of me.

Finally capturing the power and wonder contained in the Bible not only awakened a passion for God's Word but also for praying. Because, friend, it is power. More powerful than a nuclear bomb–and far more constructive!

Rinse and Repeat

Now would be a good time to acknowledge that sometimes God calls us to persevere in prayer. He doesn't always answer us right away. I know, I know. Super frustrating. And frankly, it can get boring repetitively bringing the same request to him over and over. But if we go expecting that he'll answer, it gives us the strength to push through any moments of boredom realizing that he is, in fact, listening. His answer could be on the other side of our very next prayer!

In his excellent book, *With Christ in the School of Prayer,* author Andrew Murray teaches us how to approach God and stay persistent until he answers. He says, "He [Christ] would tell us that we are not to rest without an answer, because it is the will of God, the rule in the Father's family. . . . If no answer comes, we are not to sit down in idleness that calls itself resignation and suppose that it is not God's will to give an answer. No, there must be something in the prayer that is not as God would have it . . . we must seek for grace to pray so that the answer may come. It is far easier for the flesh to submit without the answer than to yield itself to be searched and purified by the Spirit, until it has learned to pray the prayer of faith."[1]

A good father doesn't ignore his kids, and God is the best Father. So we should expect an answer. This very sense of expectation and belief in the goodness of God can help us keep boredom at bay. We'll talk more about this in chapter six when we unpack God's silence, but I wanted to touch on the fact that sometimes we don't do ourselves any favors by avoiding boredom at all costs. Sometimes we need to press into boredom and persevere. Because on the other side of a faithful, persistent, God-honoring petition is God's answer and the chance to grow. But I'll be the first to admit it can be really hard to live this out. That's why the rest of this chapter is dedicated to helping you defeat boredom with some simple strategies.

Practically Speaking

Now that we've cleared the big, mental rocks out of our way (some of those were kind of heavy, right?), it's time to break out some boredom busters. God's Word tells us to knock and keep knocking (Matt. 7:7-8). I often find it's in the moments when I need to carry the same request and burden to the Lord over and over that I could really use some help to keep going. Sometimes all we need to breathe fresh life into our prayers are some immensely practical tips. It's time to unpack my boredom-kicking strategies! When we want to break out of a rut in other areas of our lives, what do we do? We do something different. It's time to shake things up!

Tool #1: Journaling

I can hear some of you now, moaning and grousing. *Not journaling, I hate journaling!!* I used to be an enthusiastic member of your ranks. For most of my life I've listened to people rhapsodize over journaling and I just didn't see the appeal. So many people had suggested it, but I just didn't know how to do it. All of that changed when I read *The Artist's Way* by Julia Cameron. Her book revolutionized my prayer life in several very important ways. (And believe me, no one was more surprised than me to discover that I actually enjoyed journaling.)

First, journaling gave me the freedom to write without judgment, and it was not only helpful in my writing practice, but I carried it into my prayer practice too. Quite frankly, this was where it had the biggest impact. The power of Cameron's "morning pages" (which are just three pages of stream of consciousness writing first thing in the morning to shake the cobwebs out) lies in writing honest thoughts and feelings without fear of it being seen by others, making sense, or being good. She calls the practice, "brain drain, since that's one of [the] main functions."[2] Finally, I had found a workable model for journaling.

How often have you held back your true thoughts and feelings in prayer, afraid to give them voice? I know I have. Some things are just too scary to say out loud. Perhaps by writing them down, you can give them shape on the page. As I journaled, I felt fear and my inner censor slip away and an unashamed nakedness and honesty take its place.

Cameron encourages us, "There is no wrong way to do morning pages. These daily morning meanderings are not meant to be art. Or even writing . . . The morning pages will teach you to stop judging and just let yourself write . . . Three pages of whatever crosses your mind–that's all there is to it. If you can't think of anything to write, then write 'I can't think of anything to write . . .' Do this until you have filled three pages."[3] Grant yourself permission to come to the page and your prayers without holding your true self back. You'll find some incredible things there.

One of the added benefits of journaling is noticing. I'm a notoriously bad noticer. Like a lumberjack, I once split a large piece of wood that was lying in the road, ripping off my car's oil pan in the process, because I didn't notice how large it was. (And to be honest, I thought it was a small dead animal which would "give" a little if I grazed the top of it. Eww.) But back to noticing. Writing my prayers accomplishes three vital things: 1) it helps me understand what I'm truly asking God for and 2) it helps me remember what I asked for and 3) it's a written record of all the times God answered and came through. I'll be honest, I frequently feel like God isn't answering my prayers, but I feel that way far less when I write things down.

The final benefit I gained from journaling is the gift of slowing down. It takes me longer to write my prayers than to say them, which might at first seem like a good reason to take a pass on this particular tool, but it's truly a gift worth embracing. I've found that if I don't write my prayers, I can rush past the step of praying altogether. Popping off a few half formed thoughts and words, I'll convince myself that I prayed. Journaling helps me put together the words I truly mean to say, but if I'm left to say them out loud, I'll just think a few fragments of a thought and move on to the next thing for the day. Journaling helps us pause and bring our full thoughts, burdens, and joys to God.

Tool #2: Prayer Walking
(or running if that's more your thing)

In an article titled "Worn Paths" in the *Pursuit* issue of *Truly* magazine, writer Jennifer Trautmann describes the elemental way that her afternoon runs help her connect with God and process her emotions. She says, "As the first song plays, I lift and plant my heavy feet until my run becomes a prayer. My speed and stride express my anguish; my slowing expresses my willingness to listen; my stopping opens my eyes to the world around me. . . . I don't run for distance, body shape, or speed. I run to lose sight of time and meet my God in his garden of cattails, creatures, and well-worn paths."[4]

I won't deny there's power in routine, in having a set place where you consistently meet with God, but if you always pray in the same place it might be time for a change of scenery. Try prayer walking. As you strike out on your walk, use cues from nature to turn your thoughts towards God. Nearly anything in nature, be it a blade of grass sparkling with dew, or a low harvest moon so crisp it feels like you can reach out and grab it, can inspire a prayer of praise and thanksgiving.

As you concentrate on your cadence, let your breath remind you of his nearness. You can even use the practice of breath prayers as you sync your breath and stride to what the Spirit of God is doing in you. The essence of a breath prayer is to quiet yourself enough to acknowledge the One who gives you breath and your deep dependence on him to sustain it. I love this beautiful description from Mark Batterson in *Win the Day*. He says, "Some Hebrew scholars believe that the name of God, *Yahweh*–YHWH without the vowels–is the sound of breath. . . . On one hand, his name is too sacred to pronounce. On the other hand, it's whispered with every breath we take. It's our first word, our last word, and every word in between."[5]

Perhaps a change in scenery and pace will beat back boredom and help you find renewed energy and joy in prayer.

Tool #3: Make a Prayer List

Chances are, you have grocery lists, honey-do lists, and you might already have some prayer lists. But I'd like to challenge you to make a different kind of prayer list. A God-sized prayer list. Pick three things that seem impossible and unlikely, write them down, and start praying about them. Be as specific and detailed as you can.

After my grandparents passed, I remember talking with my dad about our inheritance. As we were discussing it, I quickly interjected, "But I don't expect anything." Turning to me, he said, "You should, you're family." I was stunned when I realized I carried this same attitude into my relationship with God. I didn't expect anything from him. Somehow I had convinced myself I was doing God a noble favor by keeping my expectations of him low or nonexistent, all the while he was thinking, "You should expect a lot. You're family." We expect far less than God wants us to, so we pray boring prayers that don't affect much in our present lives and certainly not eternity. It's time to get our hopes and our expectations up.

Perhaps you're bored because you're praying boring prayers. As we wrap up this chapter, I want to leave you with this question: If God answered your last three prayers, would it make much of a difference in your life? In the lives of people around you? In the world?

*Father, reveal any hidden, unexamined attitudes
I might have about prayer that are keeping me stuck
and making me feel bored. Help me understand and
embrace how powerful talking to you truly is.
Teach me how to rightly evaluate my prayer time
with you regardless of how I feel in the moment.
Help me raise my expectations. Let the prayers I
pray make a difference in the world around me.
Amen.*

Breakthrough Exercises

1. Pick one of the three tools (journaling, prayer walking, making a prayer list) and try it for at least one week consistently. Be sure to make note of how it affects your prayer life.

2. Take a moment to pinpoint one hidden thought or attitude you have about prayer. It could be one from the list in this chapter or God may have brought something else to your mind. Use this time to talk to him about it and discover what it might be telling you about your beliefs about prayer.

3. If, as you read this chapter, you realized you struggle with a spirit of disbelief, meditate on this verse until the wonder and awe of it settles into your heart and mind. "The Spirit of God, who raised Jesus from the dead, *lives in you.*" (Romans 8:11 NLT, emphasis added)

4. Because we can often make prayer about us, spend the next several minutes listing at least five attributes of God and then thank him for his flawless nature.

Hang-Up #5: Why Can't I Stay Focused?

Overcoming Distractions

CHAPTER FIVE

Squirrel

"So many people feel that if their prayer is distracted it cannot be pleasing to God, and are therefore led to abandon their efforts precisely when fidelity is of the most importance."

– SHEILA CASSIDY

As I was typing this chapter today, my cell phone was exploding with text messages. *Ding! Ding! Ding! Ding!* Group text messages (insert eye roll here). Every time I started to get into a rhythm, another ding brought my thoughts to a screeching halt. Ugh!

If there was a top ten list for the most frustrating parts of prayer, distractions would most certainly slide into one of the top slots. As I've talked with people, it's one of the issues mentioned most often. Few things are more irritating than finally finding the time to pray, only to have your mind wander like a dandelion seed caught in a strong southern breeze. But what if instead of being flustered, you could learn to embrace these unwelcome intruders? What if instead of being derailed by distractions, you were directed by them? What if you could learn to use distractions as fuel for your prayers rather than feeling frustrated by them?

This probably sounds ridiculous and too good to be true, kind of like those infomercials that suck you in at one a.m. promising that you'll look like a sixteen-year-old again. (Spoiler alert–it won't work, but going to sleep might help in that department.) But stick with me because it's not only possible for you to overcome one of the most common issues with prayer, it's completely probable with a couple of tricks up your sleeve.

Managing Expectations

Several years ago I looked at my husband and said, "I think I need glasses." To which he immediately responded, "I could have told you that. You picked me!" In all seriousness, things had been looking a little blurry, and I knew it was time to acknowledge one of the unfortunate signs of aging.

I'll never forget how amazed I was the first time I slipped those frames on my face. The world was crisper, brighter. I hadn't even noticed how much I'd been squinting. I was shocked by the difference it made in my vision. The purpose of glasses is to help you see better, but I wasn't expecting the drastic change they brought to my vision. I was surprised by their effectiveness, but I shouldn't have been. That's what they were designed to do.

Much like my experience with glasses, all too often I'm surprised by distractions when I sit down to pray, but I shouldn't be. I don't think I've had a single prayer session where I wasn't distracted or unfocused at some point or another. Distractions have earned a reputation for being the mortal enemy of our prayer lives (and they certainly can be); so it's no wonder we feel defeated when they come clattering into our brains when we're talking to God. And they always come. Every. Single. Time. So I started to wonder, if a Harvard study acknowledges that people's minds are unfocused and wandering forty-seven percent of the time,[1] *Why in the world did I keep coming to prayer expecting to be distraction free?* I was setting myself up to feel like a failure. Before we go any further, repeat this to yourself right now, as many times as you need to until it actually sinks in, "I'm going to get distracted. It's part of praying, not an indication that I'm failing." Distractions will come (they're as sure as getting sucked into another group text message). It's how we react to them that matters.

For me, one of the most persistent problems with distractions was the old voice of self-condemnation and perfectionism that crept in whispering, *You're never going to stay focused. You should just go ahead and give up. This is a battle you always lose.* On and on this voice rang in my head, every time I settled in to pray.

Maybe it sounds familiar to you too, and you're tempted to agree, because some of it is true. Distractions *are* part of the fabric of our prayer lives and we're not doing ourselves any favors by trying to deny it. In order to stop them completely, we'd have to stop praying. And we don't want to do that! Finally accepting the fact that my distractions weren't going away is what led me to discover the key that would transform them from a frustrating problem into a manageable (even useful) tool.

Learning to manage my expectations is a recurring theme in my life. Jesus and I talk about it often. You would think midway through my life that I wouldn't need to keep learning the same lessons over and over again, but apparently I'm a slow learner. Discouragement about my prayer life grew in the space between my expectations and my experiences. Slowly, it dawned on me that I created these great expectations for myself (i.e. no distractions are going to stop my prayers) and low expectations for God. We talked about this in the last chapter. Instead, I should have flipped this paradigm, saving my great expectations for God and creating realistic expectations for myself.

The "Aha!" moment that finally led me to victory over distractions was found in managing my expectations and training myself to expect them. Anticipating distractions keeps us from being derailed by them when they pop up, and also helps us prepare to use them to our advantage. When we train ourselves to count on distractions and learn to use them as fuel for our prayers, it sets us up for a much better experience. But how, exactly, do we do this?

Bring it On

Distractions have tied me in knots for *years*. It wasn't until I heard a podcast with John and Lisa Bevere that I realized this didn't have to be the case. In an off-hand comment, John tossed out the idea that we can ask God to sanctify our imaginations and direct our prayers through our wandering minds.[2] It was like a literal light bulb went on over my head; distractions don't have to be our enemy. Instead, we can allow God to lead us through them. Get out of town! What a revelation!

Sometimes all it takes to see a huge shift is a small perspective change. Nothing may actually change at all except your thinking, but that simple shift somehow transforms and touches everything. That's exactly what embracing this philosophy can do for your prayer life. Here's a perfect example. How many times has a person crossed your mind that you haven't thought about, or even seen, in years? What I used to view as a distraction and tried to push out of my mind to get back to "more important things," I've started to view as an invitation to pray. I believe these moments and thoughts are divine nudges for us to pray for specific people or things. Paul actually talks about this in Philippians 1:3 when he says, "Every time I think of you, I give thanks to my God." Whenever he thinks of them, he prays.

As often as I can, whenever someone (or something) pops into my head, I pray for them. I'd love to share a dramatic story about this. Like a moment where I prayed and then received news that a missionary's life was spared as a result or someone was miraculously healed, but I don't have any stories like that (although I've heard some pretty amazing ones). But I still believe each prayer matters, and God is keeping track. Maybe we will hear some incredible stories when we get to heaven someday!

As you start to embrace this practice, you'll experience less frustration and more freedom. When we choose to view distractions as a way for the Holy Spirit to guide our prayers, then we can rejoice at the interruptions instead of being irritated or deflated by them. This is the secret that transforms distractions from a dirty word into divine direction.

So far we've talked about unbidden thoughts that pop up like weeds in the garden of our minds, but there's another facet of transforming our distractions to explore. We can actually invite the distractions. In case you're thinking I sound genuinely crazy, and you're muttering, "There's enough distractions rolling around in my head; I don't need to go inviting more," hear me out.

It's a radical idea, I know, but you can move beyond just tolerating distractions–you can invite them. But why would you want to do that, you might be wondering? View it as yet another way to invite God's direction and presence into your prayer time.

There's a Gaelic practice called "quietness without loneliness" that I first heard of in *The Creative Habit* by Twyla Tharp, and I've co-opted it for our purposes. It's a practical way to redeem our distractions and let the Holy Spirit guide our prayers. As Tharp describes it, it's the opposite of emptying our minds in meditation, instead it's more like "active daydreaming."[3] This process asks us to allow and follow our wandering thoughts until they strike upon something that shines with the fingerprints of God. Her encouragement is to start with a short period of time and work your way up to longer periods of daydreaming with a goal in mind.

Perhaps as you come to your time of prayer for the day, you can pause and ask God what he'd like you to pray about. Maybe he will bring a country or a person to your mind. Or perhaps he'll bring to mind a problem you've been facing. In following Tharp's approach, the Holy Spirit can guide you toward a topic of prayer for the day. There's immense power in this practice because it aligns you with the Spirit and will of God as you pray (more on this in chapter thirteen).

Post-it Prayers

Now that our goal is no longer to avoid distractions at all costs, we need to talk about those mental intrusions that most certainly are not from the Holy Spirit. Because we know those are coming too–not everything that enters our mind when we're praying is from God. As we already talked about, we're trying to keep it real and acknowledge that distractions are an inevitable part of our prayer lives. Some of those distractions we'll welcome and use as fuel for our prayers. Others, not so much. So how do we show those unhelpful intruders to the door? How can we set ourselves up for success and minimize the distractions we don't want to welcome?

Unhelpful distractions fall into two categories: external and internal. External ones are typically environmental, and can be some of the easiest to deal with. (Unless you have toddlers. If you have toddlers, all bets are off, *they will find you*. But even if you have little people about, don't be discouraged. It's only a season. I promise, it will get better. And you will eventually get five minutes to yourself again.) As we tackle these external distractions, we can do things to set ourselves up for success; we can put away our cell phones and find a quiet place where people won't interrupt us. I've always hated the term prayer closet, probably because I hate dark, confined spaces, but I think there's a reason why, for centuries, people have wanted one. No one's going to bother you there! But you might not want to go there either, and that's a problem. You need to find a place where people won't bother you, but you actually enjoy going. Nearly any environmental issue can be solved with enough creative thinking and the will to make it happen.

But what about those persistent distractions that bog us down every time we sit down: those internal distractions? The ones that most certainly are *not* useful for directing our prayer time. The grocery list, the appointment we need to schedule, or the rehashing of the argument we had with our spouse for which we just came up with the most brilliant comeback? As my friend Carolyn taught me, the Post-it note is the anecdote. Whenever an errant thought enters her mind while she's praying, she takes out her stack of handy-dandy Post-it notes (which she keeps close by when she prays) and scribbles the thought down. This allows her to stay focused in the moment and not have to worry that she'll forget the thought. (Although it might be good if you let that zinger for your spouse go.) She writes it down and then anything important that needs to be tended to is waiting for her to deal with *after* she prays.

On the surface, distractions can seem like a raging forest fire, burning through your prayer time and reducing it to ash. But as we've explored them further, I hope you've discovered that they can be redeemed and repurposed. Forest fires are interesting phenomena. Yes, they can be deadly and dangerous, but they can also bring new life, fertilizing the ground for new growth and fresh starts. Some plants and trees even require the heat of fire to bloom and grow.[4] In the same way, I hope you've gained a newfound appreciation for the paradox of distractions, and they've led you to beautiful

new prayers and more opportunities for fresh encounters
with the Holy Spirit.

*Father, help me shift my heart and mind when it
comes to distractions. Help me not to beat myself up
over them, but instead lean into you and be curious
about how you might be directing me through them
towards something you'd like me to pray about.
When I'm tempted to be frustrated or give up
because of persistent distractions, help me
use them to connect with you more.*
Amen.

Breakthrough Exercises

1. Do you struggle more with internal or external distractions? What's one specific thing you can do to transform your distraction into something useful for your prayer life?

2. Make a list of your most common distractions during prayer. Can you see an intersection between those thoughts or things and something God might be leading you to pray about?

3. Tell God the thing you're most embarrassed or ashamed of, or irritated or worried about. Be specific. Tell him the details. And if you find this hard to do, remind yourself he already knows anyway.

Hang-up #4: Why Isn't God Answering Me?

Overcoming Disappointment

CHAPTER SIX

Silent

"When God is silent, He is not still."
– TONY EVANS

Silence is not golden. Whoever said that lied. Few things are as frustrating in life as the silent treatment. The longer it rages on, the deeper the rivers of suspicion and anger bubble. I was raised in a house where silence was wielded like a weapon of subtle, but powerful, destruction. Weeks, and sometimes a month or more, would slip by, as stony silence draped our house in tension and slowly simmering anger. Each silent day only brought more sour feelings and distance to traverse.

Intentional silence breeds resentment. As damaging as the silent treatment can feel in our earthly relationships, God's silence can be more damaging still. There's a whole different level of pain to be experienced when it seems like the God of the universe is freezing you out. Letting you down. Indifferent and deaf toward your prayers. Leaving you holding the broken bits of your heart and life, wondering when (or if) he's ever going to answer.

Maybe you've cried out in desperation asking, "Why hasn't God healed my alcoholic father?" or "What am I supposed to do with my impossible co-worker?" only to be greeted with overwhelming silence. These seasons of interminable waiting can breed resentment and distrust and cause us to question or lose faith.

We all face seasons where God seems silent. It's inescapable. The all-consuming question of the hour becomes how do we respond when he doesn't answer the way we would like? Or when it seems like he doesn't hear us at all? How do we learn to trust that God is doing something, most likely incredible things, when it looks like he's not doing anything? How do we keep praying and talking to him when there's no evidence to support that it's doing any good? Or, God forbid, things just keep getting worse?

Dallas Willard encouraged us to, "Never believe anything bad about God."[1] But sometimes . . . oh, sometimes that's much easier said than done.

Sucked Under by Sadness

For most of my life I've been guilty of immediately questioning and suspecting God's motives and actions, or inaction, as the case may seem. The legal standard, "Innocent until proven guilty," did not apply when it came to my opinions and judgments on God. My first inclination is not to give God the benefit of the doubt; it's to, as one of my former pastors, Glenn Reynolds, used to say, "Doubt he has any benefit." I don't know why it's always been so hard for me to trust God. This has been a lifelong struggle for me, and one I still wrestle with from time to time. Perhaps you too have faced this issue? Maybe you're facing it now?

Stuck inside my own head, struggling with God's silence, I'm sometimes shocked when I stumble across others who are dealing with the same emotions. Nearly every time I've felt like God was slighting me or ignoring me, my mind immediately shouted, *You're the only one! No one else has ever experienced this before. If you talk about this with anyone, especially God, you'll be rejected.*

Adding isolation to feelings of being ignored is a recipe for disaster. I've found it whips up cakes of confusion and cynicism and stacks of suspicion. As Lysa TerKeurst says in *It's Not Supposed to be This Way,* "If the enemy [Satan] can isolate us, he can influence us. . . .It's his subtle seduction to get us alone with our thoughts so he can slip in whispers that will develop our disappointments into destructive choices."[2] I've found this to be so very true over the years. Isolation typically leads me down a path toward increased anxiety and an itching sense of injustice.

In isolation, it's easy to fall for the lie that we shouldn't express how we really feel to others–and especially to God. We should just keep those bitter feelings and dark questions stuffed into the farthest corners of our heart. Exposure might make people recoil and question our salvation. So imagine my surprise when I stumbled upon a passage in the Bible that proved me dead wrong. Not only are we allowed to express our raw disappointments, frustrations, anger, and pain, but these very thoughts and feelings were uttered to Jesus's face. Contrary to what the enemy would have us believe, this is not a new or taboo sentiment at all. Let's look at a familiar passage of Scripture with a fresh set of eyes.

John 11 (CSB, emphasis added):

> "Now a man was sick, Lazarus from Bethany, the village of Mary and her sister Martha. Mary was the one who anointed the Lord with perfume and wiped his feet with her hair; and it was her brother Lazarus who was sick. So the sisters sent a message to him: 'Lord, the one you love is sick.'

> "When Jesus heard it, he said, 'This sickness will not end in death but is for the glory of God, so that the Son of God may be glorified through it.' *Now Jesus loved Martha, her sister, and Lazarus.* **So when he heard that he was sick, he stayed two**

more days in the place where he was. Then after that, he said to the disciples, 'Let's go to Judea again . . .'"

Time-out. This is such a strange passage that seems to hold some serious contradictions. It says plainly that Jesus loved Martha, Mary, and Lazarus, but when he heard that Lazarus was sick, he chose to stay where he was. *For two days.* To me, this seems like the opposite of love. When you love someone and they're near death, you rush to their side. Neither oceans or traffic will keep you away. So when Jesus chose to stay put, it was very curious and could come across as uncaring. Let's keep reading, because in this very next part of the passage we get some very important insight into Jesus's motives. Hint: there's always more to the story.

> "He said this, and then he told them, 'Our friend Lazarus has fallen asleep, but I'm on my way to wake him up.' Then the disciples said to him, 'Lord, if he has fallen asleep, he will get well.'

> Jesus, however, was speaking about his death, but they thought he was speaking about natural sleep. So Jesus told them plainly, 'Lazarus has died. *I'm glad for you that I wasn't there so that you may believe. But let's go to him. . .'"*

Verse 14 from *The Message* makes his purpose even clearer:

"Then Jesus made it plain to them, 'Lazarus is dead. And for your sake, I'm glad I wasn't there, because now you have another opportunity to see who I am *so that you will learn to trust in me.* Come, let's go and see him . . .'"

This passage clearly states that Lazarus's death was an opportunity for many people's faith and trust in Jesus to increase. But we're about to see what Mary and Martha thought about Jesus's delay. Let's pick back up in verse 17:

"When Jesus arrived, he found that Lazarus had already been in the tomb four days. Bethany was near Jerusalem (less than two miles away). Many of the Jews had come to Martha and Mary to comfort them about their brother.

As soon as Martha heard that Jesus was coming, she went to meet him, but Mary remained seated in the house. Then Martha said to Jesus, '*Lord, if you had been here, my brother wouldn't have died.* Yet even now I know that whatever you ask from God, God will give you.'"

Time-out again. The pain lacing Martha's words is sharp, "If only you had been here, Jesus. But you weren't. I thought you loved us. I thought you would come through." Her disappointment and bewilderment are palpable. But even in the midst of that pain and sorrow, she's still clinging to a trace of wild hope. As someone who has felt these emotions and asked similar questions of God, I feel for her.

Let's keep going.

> "'Your brother will rise again,' Jesus told her.
>
> Martha said to him, 'I know that he will rise again in the resurrection at the last day.'
>
> Jesus said to her, 'I am the resurrection and the life. The one who believes in me, even if he dies, will live. Everyone who lives and believes in me will never die. Do you believe this?'
>
> 'Yes, Lord,' she told him, 'I believe you are the Messiah, the Son of God, who comes into the world.'"

It's worth noting that even in the middle of this huge loss, Martha is rehearsing what she knows to be true about Jesus and confessing it out loud. It's clear from this conversation that Martha and Mary still had no idea what Jesus was up to. They didn't know how this story would end, but their belief in God remained strong, even as they wrestled with their grief and sadness.

> "Having said this, she went back and called her sister Mary, saying in private, 'The Teacher is here and is calling for you.'

As soon as Mary heard this, she got up quickly and went to him. Jesus had not yet come into the village but was still in the place where Martha had met him. The Jews who were with her in the house consoling her saw that Mary got up quickly and went out. They followed her, supposing that she was going to the tomb to cry there.

As soon as Mary came to where Jesus was and saw him, she fell at his feet and told him, 'Lord, if you had been here, my brother would not have died!'

When Jesus saw her crying, and the Jews who had come with her crying, *he was deeply moved in his spirit and troubled.* 'Where have you put him?' he asked.

'Lord,' they told him, 'come and see.'

Jesus wept.

So the Jews said, 'See how he loved him!' But *some of them said, 'Couldn't he who opened the blind man's eyes also have kept this man from dying?'*

Then Jesus, deeply moved again, came to the tomb. It was a cave, and a stone was lying against it. 'Remove the stone,' Jesus said.

Martha, the dead man's sister, told him, 'Lord, there is already a stench because he has been dead four days.'

Jesus said to her, 'Didn't I tell you that if you believed you would see the glory of God?'

So they removed the stone. Then Jesus raised his eyes and said, 'Father, I thank you that you heard me. I know that you always hear me, but because of the crowd standing here I said this, *so that they may believe you sent me.*' After he said this, he shouted with a loud voice, 'Lazarus, come out!' The dead man came out bound hand and foot with linen strips and with his face wrapped in a cloth. Jesus said to them, 'Unwrap him and let him go.'"

Right about now you might be thinking, *Well, that's a good story with a happy ending. What about the stories that don't end with resurrection, Erica?* The pain of loss and the sting of disappointment stuns us not because we don't believe Jesus can heal and deliver and set all things right; it comes because we know he can and we just don't understand why sometimes he doesn't. I've been guilty of echoing the words of the Jewish bystanders who said, "Couldn't he who opened the blind man's eyes also have kept this man from dying?" Their words drip with cynicism, but probably also hide deep disappointment and sadness.

You hear the unmasked emotion in the voices of Mary and Martha as they greet Jesus, "If you'd been here this never would have happened." There's an unspoken question, "Where were you when we needed you? It feels like you've let us down. You could have spared us all this pain, but you didn't. Why?"

I'm so grateful that God gave us these honest stories, full of in-the-moment reactions and raw feelings because when God is silent we're tempted to believe two things: 1) that he's ignoring us, and if his silence continues for any length of time 2) that he's abandoned us and doesn't care. We saw it in the passage we just read from John 11, and we also see it in David's cry to God in Psalm 66. He says:

> "But God *did* listen! He paid attention to my prayer. Praise God, who did not ignore my prayer or withdraw his unfailing love from me." (Psalm 66:19-20 NLT, emphasis added)

It's as if David is relieved. *Oh! God* didn't *ignore me. He does still love me! Whew! You had me worried there for a minute, God.* This verse tells us plainly that God doesn't ignore our prayers and he won't remove his love from us. But how do we hold these truths in our minds and hearts when our emotions threaten to pin us under an avalanche of grief, erasing every possibility of rational thought?

Waiting Well

Apparently I've been impatient for quite some time. One of my earliest everyday memories of my grandpa was him chiding me to be patient (and me thinking he needed to take his own advice). Most of us could use a little extra practice in this category–but none of us want it.

More often than not, our frustration with God's silence comes after we've persistently carried our burdened souls to Jesus and . . . nothing's happened. We've waited, we've pleaded, we've worn our voices scratchy and poured out all our tears. What then?

"God, where are you? Don't you care? I've been praying for this forever, and nothing has happened. Am I just wasting my breath? Why won't you answer me," we wail, right before we just stop asking. This is such a tender topic because waiting is hard and silence feels personal.

When we've emptied the Kleenex boxes over our addicted mother, or our broken marriage, or our wayward kids, and the only answer for our grief is silence, it's enough to make you wanna cuss.

Which reminds me of a man in the Bible, Job, who was experiencing God's silence and his wife advised him to curse God and die (Job 2:9). Definitely not the greatest advice, but when you see what happened to him, you can understand where she's coming from. He lost his children, his livelihood, and finally, his health. Yet Job refused to curse God, because he understood three things:

- He couldn't accept God's blessings without also accepting trouble (2:10).
- He would have nothing without God (1:21).
- He was not fit or qualified to judge God (38:4-7).

I'll be honest, even though I agree with each of these statements intellectually, and I've found all of them to be true at various points in my life, the ending of the book of Job just doesn't sit right with me. I still wonder why Job's children died. Did the end really justify the means? Only God knows. And only God knows the answers to the questions I'm asking today and his perfect timing for my life as well. And yet, I so foolishly think *I* know better. In my impatience and anger, I feel so justified sitting on my little throne judging God. Slamming my gavel down, I render my verdict. Unjust. *Bang!* Unfair. *Bang!* Uncaring. *Bang!* At the heart of all of my judgment, perhaps, is the idea that I'm owed better. That somehow I don't deserve this trial, this sickness, this silence.

When my husband and I were missionaries in India, he became extremely sick with dysentery. (I'm going to confess right here that I hadn't heard that word since elementary school when I used to play a game called "Oregon Trail" on an enormous computer and all my players kept dying from it!) Some friends of ours came over to lay hands on him and pray for healing. Lifting their voices, one of them said, "God, please heal our friend. He's sacrificed so much to be here serving you; heal him and make him well." The implication in the prayer was that because we were spending our lives in a "sacrificial" way that God owed us good health. Honestly, that didn't sit right. Deep down we know that God doesn't owe us anything, that he's already done more than enough for us. And yet . . . we also have this deep desire for fairness. Justice. Missionaries getting sick offended my friend's sense of fairness. And while I knew it wasn't right for me to expect perfect health as a missionary, there are other areas where God offends my sense of equity. I may know in my head that it's not rational, but I just don't care.

I really don't know if I'll ever get over the knee-jerk instinct to judge and blame God when he doesn't do what I ask of him when I ask him to do it. When he chooses to be silent. Or when he does finally answer and it just doesn't satisfy my sense of fairness or justice. I've been on this ride enough times to know that if I can stand outside of my pain and questions for even just a moment, I get enough clarity to see that God is in fact, oh so very just. And kind. Unfortunately, it usually requires hindsight for me to recognize his hand at work, transforming terrible things and working them for my ultimate good. It's usually so hard, if not impossible, to recognize it in the middle of hurt and long seasons of waiting.

I have no easy answers for this issue of silence, except to take slow, steady steps towards trust. That was the purpose of Lazarus's death and resurrection; Jesus spelled that out clearly to his disciples and, in turn, to us thousands of years later. His voice echoes through the ages reminding us, "You can trust me."

Could it be that Jesus's delay in answering your question or prayer could be meant as an opportunity for you to reach a bone-deep level of belief? Could he have gone to Lazarus immediately and kept him from dying? Of course! But he would have short-circuited an even greater plan that resulted in countless people coming to faith in God. Perhaps there's a greater purpose to your season of waiting than you could ever imagine.

We can look at the lives of Job, Mary, and Martha and see a model of what to do while we're waiting, how to take those small steps towards trust. Job poured out his pure, unfiltered thoughts and feelings to God. His life is proof that in moments of crisis, when God seems silent, it's time to go to him more. It's tempting to want to shut down and push God out. Even though it goes against every human instinct, it's time to double down, not clam up.

And just like Mary and Martha, we need to rehearse what we know to be true about God. In moments of pain, it's easier to rehearse our injuries and offenses, wallowing in our feelings instead of trusting in the truth of God's character and his Word.

After years of utterly failing at this, I'm finally learning that it's the moments where I feel like rehearsing God's faithfulness the least that I need the reminder the most. Those are precisely the moments where I need to get out my journal and recount all the times God has shown up in my life. The instances are countless, but I'm a forgetful person, prone to angry accusations and disappointed demands. Mary and Martha remind us that rehearsing God's faithfulness is where we regain hope in the midst of hopeless situations.

In the waiting, it can be easy to panic and think God is taking too long, therefore he must not be doing anything, so we should probably take matters into our own hands. The people of Israel give us a cautionary tale in Exodus 32. When they saw that Moses was taking forever on the mountain with God, they started to freak out and they said to Aaron, "Who even knows if that Moses guy is coming back! He's been gone for AGES!! (This is the New Erica Paraphrase.) Make us a god that we can see, feel and touch."

What's especially crazy about this story is that God was literally on the mountain with Moses promising to dwell among the people of Israel. He was promising his actual presence in their midst. God was in the middle of giving Moses instructions to make the tabernacle that would be the place where God would meet with the children of Israel and live with them, but they were too impatient to wait for it. They thought they knew better.

I can be so judgmental when it comes to the Israelites, imagining myself to be so much holier, but when it comes down to it, I'm not that different. This story is such a great picture of how we respond when we have to wait. We settle for a counterfeit, something we can manufacture with our own hands, when the promise, God's presence and provision, is literally on the way down the mountain.

So if you find yourself in a season where God seems silent, hold on, my friend. His answer is coming down the mountain. You might be wondering how I can say that. Again, I'll point back to our friend, Job. Even though he had to wait for what probably seemed like an eternity for a response from

God, it did come. As I said in a previous chapter, God doesn't ignore his kids.

And if you could use even more assurance, take a look at this passage from Exodus 2. When I read it in *The Message* it practically popped off the page into my eyeballs and settled deep into my heart. Since I've often accused God of ignoring me or not caring, it's as if he set these verses in front of me and said, "See, *this* is what I do when you pray." And it's the complete opposite of all that I've always accused him of. Exodus 2:23-25 says: "God listened . . . God remembered . . . God saw . . . and God understood."

He heard their deep groanings, he remembered his promises, he looked at their situation, and he understood their suffering. I don't know about you, but seeing that in black and white does something for my heart, and I hope it does for you as well.

The Bee in My Bonnet

Before we move on from this topic, we need to talk about one more thing. Because I've got a lot of issues, and one of them is "Susie." You know her. Everybody knows a Susie. She's the one everyone goes to for prayer. It seems like she has a direct line to the ear of God. Her prayers always get answered–the first time. There's no waiting or having to constantly remind herself of God's faithfulness–or so it seems. Just pure, unadulterated answered prayer. And legitimately, I rejoice for Susie. But I'm also a little miffed by her.

Maybe it sounds like I'm being funny, and I am a little bit. It's actually nothing personal against "Susie," but she dredges up all of my insecurities and feelings of inferiority about prayer. She makes me wonder, *Does God just like some people more? Is that why they always seem to get an answer to their prayer–and usually the one they want?* Having a Susie around can be especially painful if you've been waiting for what seems like eons for God to answer one measly request and then Susie over there gets everything she asks for–immediately. Talk about frustrating and discouraging.

But don't hate on Susie. And don't waste any more time feeling inferior to her. Here's why.

First Corinthians 12:4-11 tells us that God gives *each of us* spiritual gifts. Among them are gifts of faith, healing, and miracles, so perhaps Susie has been given one of these gifts and she is operating fully within it. We should praise the Lord for that, because he's also given each of us gifts as well. Paul goes on in that same passage to say, "A spiritual gift is *given to each of us so we can help each other*" (vs. 7 NLT, emphasis added). Which isn't to say that God can't use anyone at any time, functioning in any gift, but we need Susie. She's a blessing given to help (not irritate) the body of Christ.

As I contemplated this issue, I realized there could be another reason why it seems like Susie gets an overwhelming amount of prayers answered. Are you ready for it? As I've already confessed at the beginning of this book, I've struggled to pray for much of my life, and I believe the primary difference between me and Susie (specific spiritual gifts aside) is that while I was thinking about my prayer need or talking to someone else about it, Susie was praying. Talking to God about it. Inviting him into it.

Put simply, Susie had more answered prayers because she prayed more. To someone from the outside looking in, who doesn't see the amount of time Susie spends praying, it could probably seem like God is playing favorites, but it's actually simple math. The more you pray, the more God will answer. And as he answers, you'll naturally want to talk about what he's done! Susie was probably talking about answered prayers a lot because she was praying a lot. Which is good news for you and me. We don't have to be jealous of the Susies of the world, we can become one!

God, your silence is so hard for me to handle.
But I don't want to become cynical or bitter;
I want to trust you even when I can't understand
what's happening. Help me to be more like Job
and Mary and Martha. Help me rehearse your
faithfulness and all the things I know to be true
about your character when I'm feeling abandoned or
hopeless in my seasons of waiting. I know you're
a good Father, and you're not ignoring me.
Help me hold on until you answer.
Amen.

Breakthrough Exercises

1. Make a list of thirty things God has done that you're grateful for. Sometimes in the midst of waiting, we can feel discouraged and forgotten. Making this list will help you remember that while you may still be waiting for God to answer or show up in one area of your life, he is still with you and he's been faithful to you in the past.

2. If you're in a silent season, what would it look like for you to take a small step towards God in trust? What is one thing, no matter how small, that you can do to show God that you trust him, even while you're still waiting for him to answer.

3. Isolation is dangerous in so many areas of our lives, but especially in our walk with God. If you're in a dark season, find a friend you can talk to, *and* don't give in to the lie that you can't talk to God about how you're feeling.

Hang-up #5: What's *Really* Going on Here?
Overcoming Spiritual Battles

CHAPTER SEVEN

This is War

*"When we only accept unseen realities as entertainment
(i.e. Harry Potter and Lord of the Rings)
and fail to see them as a very real part of this
world we reject the worldview of the Bible.
We are in need of a reality check."*
– MASON KING

My husband, Jonathan, and I have very different ideas of what constitutes great television. One of the shows we disagree about most vehemently is *Finding Bigfoot*. He is so immensely entertained by the ridiculous antics of these self-proclaimed "bigfoot hunters" who travel around visiting different locations of so-called sightings, searching for evidence of the hairy sasquatch's existence. Not surprisingly, the "evidence" they find is often sketchy at best. And in all the episodes he's watched, guess what they've never actually gotten footage of? You guessed it: bigfoot.

If you're a bigfoot believer please don't be offended. But spending an hour of my life watching a TV show that ultimately ends with little to no evidence supporting that the thing they're looking for even exists leaves me feeling slightly ragey. I mean, who is bankrolling this? I've got a few ideas I'd like to pitch to them!

For years I thought about spiritual warfare and the schemes of Satan about as much as I thought about bigfoot and the Loch Ness Monster. Which is to say I thought about them never. Inadvertently, I filed spiritual forces and realities away somewhere between aliens, bigfoot, and the Loch Ness Monster (i.e. things I'd never seen or experienced in real life). I secretly wondered if Paul was being a little dramatic in Ephesians 6:12 when he said, ". . . We are not fighting against flesh and blood enemies, but against evil rulers and authorities of the unseen world, against mighty powers in this dark world, and against evil spirits in the heavenly places." I'd heard stories about people being delivered from demons and read about it in the Bible, but it seemed like something that had no real impact on my daily life. Something for super Christians and pastors to deal with. Not me. It's not that I didn't believe that demons and Satan existed; it's just that safe and comfortable in my midwestern bubble, I never had any encounters with them.

And let's just be real. There's some weirdness around spiritual warfare too, which led me to keep it at arm's length like a smelly sock. Who wants to invite weird into their life? Not me. Unfortunately, just because I chose not to acknowledge spiritual forces didn't mean they ceased to exist. On any given day I can pretend the IRS doesn't exist, and since I don't see IRS agents in my daily life, I could convince myself that they aren't real. But come April 15th, I'm very aware of their existence. In the same way, we can't see our heart beating, our brain functioning, or our bones supporting us, but these things are the very foundation of our physical bodies. Much like these unseen, but incredibly real, elements of our physical bodies the Bible tells us the unseen spiritual realm is just as real.

I'll be honest, this is not my favorite chapter to write. I prefer to avoid negative things and pretend they don't exist. If I had a spirit animal it would be an ostrich. Maybe it's the Enneagram seven in me–the Enthusiast. An eternal optimist, I choose to look at the positive side of life, and talking about fighting battles and Satan attacking me is not at the top of my list of positive things to think about. You know what I mean? So in true ostrich fashion, I buried my head in the sand and just didn't think about it. Honestly, for years that worked pretty well for me. Or at least I thought it did.

So what changed? In a word, India. It wasn't until we moved to India as missionaries that it became crystal clear exactly what Paul was talking about in Ephesians when he said, "Finally, let the mighty strength of the Lord make you strong. Put on all the armor that God gives, so you can defend yourself against the devil's tricks. We are not fighting against humans. We are fighting against forces and authorities and against rulers of darkness and powers in the spiritual world. So put on all the armor that God gives. Then when that evil day comes, you will be able to defend yourself. And when the battle is over, you will be standing firm."[1]

Notice Paul said "when" not "if." Spiritual attack is coming, because the spirit realm is real. Praying is hard because the enemy of our soul doesn't want us talking with God. Our spiritual adversary knows that prayer changes things–and it changes us. So he fights us with all the power of hell, trying to keep us blind to his schemes and his existence, lulling us into complacency so he can wreak havoc without our interference. Spiritual warfare could be the most likely, and most overlooked, reason why you don't pray. Satan is scared of your prayers. Or more accurately, he's afraid of the power of God released on the world when you pray. So if he can stop you, you better believe he will. Using any and every means available to him.

So, just like Paul says in Ephesians, we need to be pre-pared, but we don't have to get weird and we don't need to be afraid. Satan and his demons are no match for our God. But you do need to be aware. If the devil can catch you with your guard down, unaware of his very existence, he's got you right where he wants you. And I can tell you from experience that's a dangerous place to live.

Awake and Aware

When I gave birth to my first child, Jacob, I had not one clue about much of anything when it came to babies. One area where I was completely caught off guard was how much they pooped. Before Jacob the word "blowout" meant a flat tire or shiny hair. It was about to take on a whole new meaning. A couple of days after he was born we took him to the doctor's office for a checkup, and I forgot the diaper bag. More accurately, I left the diaper bag at home. Since the doctor's office was only a few minutes away from our house, I thought, *We won't need this. We'll be home in thirty minutes.* All the experienced moms are chuckling right now. Rookie mistake, I know. Let's just say, there was a need for that diaper bag. A huge need.

When the nurse walked in and found a flustered mom holding a naked baby, begging for a diaper, she responded as any seasoned mother would, "Where's your diaper bag?" Fighting back tears and deep feelings of embarrassment and inadequacy I squeaked out, "I didn't think I'd need it." She quickly pointed out the error of my ways and instructed me to never leave home without a diaper bag again. Let's just say I did not readily receive her words as the pearls of wisdom they were, but I did heed her unsolicited advice and never left the house again without the diaper bag in tow.

As a new mom I was completely unaware of so many things. While that's a funny story and we can have a laugh at my expense, when we're caught unaware spiritually the consequences are far more dire than a ruined outfit and a few tears. Like so many things, I learned this lesson the hard way as India schooled me in the realities of the unseen spirit realm.

Never was the existence of dark spiritual forces more obvious or tangible than during our time in India. From the moment we stepped off the plane, there was a palpable heaviness that settled over us. Darkness, usually just something we saw with our eyes, was something we could feel in our spirits as our car slipped past the shrines devoted to hundreds of different Hindu gods. The atmosphere smacked of spirituality, but was suspiciously absent of the Spirit and presence of God.

Not long into our time in a small Himalayan village, I began to unravel mentally. My usually sunny personality turned sour and dark, plagued by irrational thoughts and insomnia. Each morning that I could drag myself out of bed, I trudged up the mountainside to language school, attempting to twist my tongue and discipline my brain to learn new sounds and words. With each passing week, I sunk deeper and deeper into anxiety and depression.

After a few short months, I found myself staring down a mountainside dotted with ancient pine trees seriously considering taking my own life. *How did I get there?* I wondered. I had never struggled with suicidal thoughts before. But after just a few short months in India, I was undone. Completely broken and unable to think straight. No longer recognizable to myself.

During that time, a much more spiritually aware friend told me about another friend of hers, living in a different city in India. She had a cross in her front yard, and one day a snake came and started striking at it. Grasping the blatant symbolism, I got the chills but laughed it off thinking, *Some people really get into that stuff.*

Not until I left that village and met with a counselor in Thailand did it become clear that I was under siege, and there were very real spiritual forces that didn't want us in India. Much later I learned that my language teacher had given herself over to demon possession at a festival in Varanasi. She was famous throughout the village for the power she wielded through demonic spirits she had invited into her life. And I had no idea. Every day I sat under her influence as she taught me Hindi, and I was vulnerable because I was clueless to her spiritual state.

Before that season of my life, I would have been tempted to think that her spiritual status wouldn't have any effect on me. That I was somehow immune because of the power and presence of God in me. But friend, let me tell you, it had an effect. A devastating one. Because I was completely unaware and unprepared to fight the spiritual battle in front of me. Daily exposure to those spiritual influences while being unaware and unguarded was very unwise.

Please don't misunderstand what I'm saying. My battle was not with my language teacher. Not at all. In fact, Paul makes this abundantly clear in his letter to the Ephesians. Our fight is not with people; it's with spiritual forces that are at war with God and his people. But I was completely oblivious to the fact that I was in a fight at all. The devil loves an easy target, and I was a sitting duck. Because nothing is easier to target than someone who isn't even aware that they're under attack.

Sometimes Satan tips his hand and works in obvious ways, but more often than not he's subtly devious and if we're not paying attention we won't realize what's truly going on around us. That's why it's vital that we be spiritually aware. We need to pray that the Lord will give us eyes to see and ears to hear what the Spirit is saying and the wisdom to recognize the attacks of the enemy. The Bible clearly tells us, "Be on your guard and stay awake. Your enemy, the devil, is like a roaring lion, sneaking around to find someone to attack."[2]

If we go through life with our heads in the sand, thinking spiritual warfare and the devil are just a bit of mythical folklore or nothing that we need to concern ourselves with, it's quite possible we'll miss what's actually happening in the realm of the spirit. We'll go through life being the victim of Satan's schemes instead of the victorious warrior that God has given us the power to be.

In no way am I saying there's a demon around every corner or the devil is behind every bad day, but are you aware that there might be more happening beyond the surface of your circumstances than what meets the eye? Are you asking God to show you what's going on? Are you asking him to give you eyes that truly see? Have you asked him to sharpen your spiritual senses? If you're serious about wanting to pray more, this is an area that you need to take seriously.

At this point, I'd like to issue a word of caution. As I said earlier, there is some real weirdness around spiritual warfare and we can easily get carried away in our zeal to be more spiritually aware. As you're becoming more sensitive to the spiritual battles taking place around you, be careful not to give the devil and his minions too much credit, or to attribute every bad circumstance to him. He's not that powerful. He is not on the same level as God. Not even close. He is not omnipresent, nor does he know everything. It can be anxiety inducing to think that he's focused on you all the time. Rest assured, he's not. Please take this as the comfort it should be–you're not that important. Even Jesus wasn't under attack from Satan every moment of his earthly ministry. Matthew 4:11 tells us that after Jesus's temptation in the wilderness, "the devil went away." Not even Jesus experienced constant attacks from Satan, so there's no need to think that you will.

As you're growing in spiritual awareness, if you're unsure if something is an attack, ask God to make it clear to you. The more your perception grows, you'll start to recognize and anticipate when Satan might attack and you won't be caught off guard as often. Becoming more spiritually aware is like building a muscle; the more you work it, the stronger it becomes.

This is How I Fight My Battles

It's one thing to be aware of spiritual battles taking place around you. A very important thing. But it's another thing entirely to fight back, to move from defense to offense. So how, exactly, do you fight against something you can't usually see, feel, or touch?

I love the way Eugene Peterson translates Ephesians 6:13-18 in *The Message.* It says, "Be prepared. You're up against far more than you can handle on your own. Take all the help you can get, every weapon God has issued, so that when it's all over but the shouting you'll still be on your feet. Truth, righteousness, peace, faith, and salvation are more than words. Learn how to apply them. You'll need them throughout your life. God's Word is an indispensable weapon. In the same way, prayer is essential in this ongoing warfare."

In this passage, Paul lays out the battle plan for us and tells us how we can fight to win every spiritual battle. The key is recognizing that this is not a physical battle so we can't fight with physical weapons. Spiritual battles must be fought with spiritual weapons. We have to begin by acknowledging that we are not equipped to fight spiritual battles without God. It's "far more than you can handle on your own."

Learning to fight spiritual battles requires that we look at spiritual practices differently. Have you ever thought of prayer as a weapon? Or the Word of God as a sword that sends the enemy packing? Maybe you've heard these phrases before and thought, *Oh, ok. But what does that even mean?* Perhaps you've read about the armor of God in Ephesians 6:13-18 and thought, *Cool, but how do I actually "put on" the armor of God? What does it look like to fight a battle with these things?*

Fortunately for us, Jesus teaches us exactly how to do it. In Matthew 4, we find him in the middle of an intense spiritual battle and feeling just a tinge hungry. He's been fasting for forty days, and Satan chooses that moment, when he's at his weakest, to go on the attack. It's worth noting that's often when Satan will attack us as well. For every temptation that the devil threw at him, Jesus responded with Scripture. Jesus had the Word of God at the ready. Every time. One practical way that you can use Scripture as your spiritual weapon is to grab a Bible with a concordance or Google some Scriptures that apply to the battle you're facing. Jesus spoke the Word of God in reply to Satan's attacks. And you know what? Satan couldn't argue with them. He knew they were true. We'll talk more about praying Scripture in chapter twelve, but for now just know that the truth of God's Word is a weapon that routs the devil every time.

The other tool that Paul says is "essential" as we fight spiritual battles is prayer. Because prayer is one of the most valuable spiritual weapons you possess, all the power of hell will rise up against you when you begin to live like you believe that's true. Praying is some of the most important work you will ever do. Stop here. Let that sink in. Prayer is not an afterthought, or a meaningless ritual. It is THE work through which God invites us to partner with him in the world. Once that truth moves past your head and sinks deep into your soul, you'll be a force to be reckoned with for the kingdom of God and a real threat and target for the enemy.

Maybe your struggle to pray is evidence that the enemy trembles over what God will unleash when you pray. If that doesn't excite you and drive you to your knees, I don't know what will. The deeper I get into prayer, the more convinced I become that it's the key to absolutely everything. That's why Satan will fight you tooth and nail if you decide to get serious about it. And the more you engage in spiritual battles, a strange thing might start to happen; you might start to view Satan's attacks as a good thing.

Be Encouraged

As I've already confessed, when I think about spiritual warfare, my mind automatically goes negative. But did you know there are some positive things to be said about it? While it can definitely be discouraging, exhausting, and hard to be under spiritual attack (if you've ever experienced intense spiritual attack you might be thinking, *That's an understatement and you're a real weirdo to suggest that there might be anything good about it*), when I was in India I began to view being a target as an honor. You see, there's no need to attack someone who isn't doing anything. During that season, I began to see spiritual attacks as confirmation that I was a threat to the enemy and his schemes–and that breakthrough was on the way.

As my spiritual awareness grew, I started to notice that the enemy always attacked most viciously right before the Lord came through with an answer to prayer or a sweet victory. Once I was wise to his schemes, it didn't make it any easier to stand firm and fight, but it did help me keep my spirits up.

So be encouraged today if you find yourself under attack. Satan wouldn't target you if he didn't see you as a threat. While this might be small comfort if you're in the midst of the fight of your life, it has encouraged me over the years and given me the stubborn resolve to dig in my heels and fight. Because you're equipped to *win* this battle, my friend. Just like *The Message* said, "When it's all over but the shouting you'll still be on your feet." Here's to being on our feet and standing strong and knocking the devil off of his game.

Father, increase my spiritual awareness.
Help me recognize the attacks of the enemy
and fight back with the tools you've given me:
your Word and my words lifted in prayer.
Strengthen me when I feel discouraged and worn
down. Remind me that it's because Satan is scared
of what you'll do when I pray.
Amen.

Breakthrough Exercises

1. Have you ever considered that the reason you struggle to pray might be due to spiritual warfare? Take a moment to ask God if this might be a reason why you find it hard to talk with him consistently.

2. Do you consider yourself spiritually aware or unaware? If you feel unaware, when you face difficulties, train yourself to ask God if there is a spiritual component to it.

3. Has it ever occurred to you that facing spiritual attack is an indication that you're making a difference in the kingdom of God? If you feel like you're experiencing an attack right now, spend some time praising God and ask him to help you stand strong.

CHAPTER EIGHT

Is That Really You, God?

*"If you do all the talking when you pray,
how will you ever hear God's answers?"*

– A.W. TOZER

Sitting under the warm sanctuary lights one early December Sunday, our guest speaker for the day directed us to a passage of Scripture. Upon reading it, I immediately felt like the Lord was pouring the words directly into my soul, each syllable soaked into my heart like rain on a sun-baked desert wasteland. I'd been seeking direction about something very specific and this felt like a clear answer to my questions. Quickly, I jotted each Scripture down knowing I might need to wait a little while for all of it to come to pass. I was thinking perhaps just a few months. It was a good thing I wrote them down, because it would be a long wait.

Countless times over the last four years, as I've waited (and am still waiting) for God to come through on what I felt he spoke to me that day, I've asked myself, "Did I really hear from God? Or did I just manufacture something that reinforced my own wants and desires and then convince myself that it was the voice of God speaking to me?"

We recognize all kinds of things by the way they sound. I can pick my husband's voice out of a crowd, and babies are said to know the sound of their mother's voice while still in the womb. We rely on our sense of hearing for so much, but what do we do when it seems unreliable? What if it's just not clear? Getting direction from God and hearing from him can feel so difficult and confusing because we seldom hear him speak out loud.

When I was a teenager we used these contraptions with long curly cords that plugged into the wall to communicate from house to house. This ancient artifact was called a landline telephone. I believe they may have one in the Smithsonian now. Many an afternoon and evening were spent with the receiver tucked against my ear talking with my best friend, Mindy. After all those hours and hours logged, I became very familiar with the sound of her voice. She never had to tell me it was her; I knew the instant I picked up the phone. No caller ID needed. One day I picked up the phone and proceeded to have a long conversation with her, or at least someone I thought was her. Midway through the conversation there were a few words that sounded just a little bit off. Suddenly, it dawned on me; I was talking to her brother. Because they sounded so similar before his voice changed, I had no idea. He tricked me into thinking I was talking to Mindy, when I'd actually been talking to him all along.

Sometimes talking with God can feel a little bit like that. We wonder if we're really hearing him or if it's someone or something else entirely, like our own thoughts and desires. Occasionally we wonder, *Is God trying to trick me?* Or, *Why did he make this so hard?* Since prayer is meant to be a conversation between you and God, this book wouldn't be complete without addressing the very important aspect of being able to hear his voice and discern when he's speaking to you. But how do we learn to trust that it's the right voice on the other end of the line and not our own heart or desires trying to trick us?

If you have more questions than answers and more confusion than clarity around this topic, you're not alone. Talking about the voice of God and hearing from him can bring up so many insecurities, even among seasoned believers–because no one gets it right all the time. So how can we know if God is really speaking to us? How do we distinguish between our own thoughts and ideas and God's voice? What does it mean when people say God spoke to them or they heard from the Lord?

Don't despair. There really are ways that you can get better at listening to God. Just like any skill we can practice and improve. As we make our way through this chapter, you'll learn how to recognize God's voice, how he speaks to you uniquely, and start to feel confident in your ability to hear and listen to him. It really is possible!

Let Me Count the Ways

Let's take a moment and acknowledge right now, hearing from God can feel very confusing and mystical. Over the years I've heard a lot of people toss around the phrase, "God told me . . ." or "God spoke to me . . ." Perhaps, like me, you've had to choke back a lump in your throat every time you've heard those words because they set off a litany of questions that rush over you like a stampede of girls when they open the doors at a women's conference. *Do they really mean that they heard the actual voice of God? Like his real out loud voice? Or did they mean something else? Am I somehow inferior if God doesn't speak to me that way?* I often wondered why some people seemed to hear from God far more than I did.

It's at this point that I'd like to say I've always been very careful about the language that I use when I talk about hearing from God. I rarely ever say, "God spoke to me." Not because the Lord doesn't speak to me, but because it really shuts down a conversation. Have you ever been talking to someone, and they completely ended all dialogue by dropping the bomb, "God told me to do this"? It's as if they just slammed on the brakes, opened the door, threw you out on the curb, and left you choking on a cloud of burnt rubber as they tore off into the night. It's kind of hard to argue with God. (And, I'll just be honest, I don't always agree that the Lord told them the things they said he did.) I'm actually pretty leery of people who casually toss around the phrase, like it's a cheap, dollar store bracelet instead of a priceless family heirloom. There's a weight that God's voice carries and it should be taken seriously.

Most of the time when God speaks to me, it's personal. It's not meant to be shared with others. So there's not a lot of need to go around saying, "God told me this . . ." or "God told me that . . ." The point of hearing from God is not to win arguments, manipulate people or situations, or to appear more spiritual. The point of hearing from God, of really listening to him, is to be in relationship with him. To follow where he's leading. To do what he asks. To be shaped and formed more and more into his likeness.

The entire story of the Bible, from cover to cover, reveals a God that pursues people. God wants to be in relationship with us, and one of the essential ingredients in any relationship is communication. Without it, the relationship breaks down and devolves into suspicion and accusation. We've been working on being able to talk with God throughout this book, but we also need to listen. Because talking to God is only half of the equation; the other half is posturing ourselves to listen. Prayer was never meant to be a monologue. How boring would that be? Although, I've definitely spent plenty of years treating it that way.

If my husband did all of the talking in our relationship and never allowed me to speak or listened to anything I said I wouldn't put up with that for long. I wouldn't feel like we were in a relationship at all–at least not a good one. Our relationship with God is no different. God wants to speak with us, but we can shy away from his voice out of fear of getting it wrong or just not knowing how to listen. It can seem intimidating to figure out how to "discern God's voice." Even using a word like "discern" makes it seem overly difficult. What does it mean to discern something anyway? Very simply, it means to "discover or uncover the truthfulness of something using wisdom and good judgment."[1] Wisdom and good judgment come from the Lord.

In order to bring some clarity and cut down on the intimidation factor around this topic, I'd like to look at a few different ways that God spoke to people in the Bible and give some practical examples. This list is not in any way exhaustive because we serve a creative God. He can speak to people in any way he chooses at any time, but let's dive in and look at a few of the ways he speaks.

Dreams and Visions

I've had some weird dreams over the years. One particularly vivid one involved a boulder-sized potato rolling over me in my front yard. Almost thirty-five years later I still remember waking up in a cold sweat, feeling like something was sitting on my chest. And then there are dreams I can't remember anything about five minutes after I wake up. It's as if their details dissolved in the steam of my shower. Dreams can be joyful, terrifying, comforting, sad. They can come from God or from the pizza you ate before bed. So how can we tell the difference? How can we know if a dream or vision came from God?

Joel 2:28 says, "...I will pour out my Spirit upon all people. Your sons and daughters will prophesy. Your old men will dream dreams, and your young men will see visions." God-given dreams and visions have a purpose. Most often it's to bring him glory. That's the entire purpose of our existence so it makes sense that when he speaks to us, through any avenue, that the ultimate purpose is to bring him glory.

My husband is a church planter, and almost five years ago our church moved from a leased facility into our own building. It was an exciting moment, but let's just say the place needed some work. After extensive renovating and remodeling, we came to the basement gym that was designated as the youth space, and we were stumped. The room was a giant concrete bowl, the stuff of insurance nightmares. Many stories had been shared of people who had fallen down the unforgiving, awkward steps, suffering the injuries to prove it. Thinking about setting teenagers loose in the space gave me hives and visions of death and cracked skulls. Definitely not the kind of visions you want to see.

It was during this time that a woman from our church told Jonathan that she had a vision about how to make the youth room functional and safe, which she proceeded to draw out on a piece of paper. Platforms were created to cover the hazardous stairs and the space was transformed into a truly exceptional room for the students to meet in. We all confirmed that her vision was from the Lord! It was an answer to a very perplexing problem, and now that space is full of students every week, enjoying it safely for the glory of God.

Insomnia

If God can speak to us through dreams, he can also speak to us during those times when sleep eludes us. In Genesis 32 we find Jacob, about to return home, and more than a little stressed about the reception he'll receive from his brother when he arrives. After a lot of plotting and planning (and extravagant gift-giving) he finally settles down for the night, but he doesn't sleep. Instead, he spends the night wrestling with God. God had instructed Jacob to return home, and yet it seemed to him like his brother might be waiting there to kill him. Had he heard God right?

In verse 9 and 12 he prays, "'O God of my grandfather Abraham, and God of my father, Isaac–O Lord, you told me,

"Return to your own land and to your relatives." And you promised me, "I will treat you kindly . . . and I will multiply your descendants until they become as numerous as the sands along the seashore–too many to count.'"

As Jacob faced this moment of confusion, where he knew God had clearly instructed him to return home, he was still wondering if he'd heard God correctly. Because it seemed like certain disaster was awaiting him there. In that moment of uncertainty, Jacob wrestled through the night with God, seeking his blessing. When we wonder if we've heard God correctly, we too can wrestle with him through the night. Sometimes the only thing to do when we can't sleep is to praise the Lord. We can have an all-night praise session and remind ourselves (and him) of his promises, and thank him that his answers are already on the way.

Impressions and Ideas

I've spent a fair amount of my life completely jealous of the patriarchs and prophets in the Bible. (I bet that's not something you hear every day.) Every time I read the words, "God spoke to Moses," a twinge of jealousy would grip me and I'd think, *If only it were that easy! Why doesn't God speak to me like that?!* I would then proceed to throw myself an elaborate pity party. But the fact is that God does speak to me, though it's usually in much subtler ways.

Outside of reading the Bible, the way God speaks to me most often is through impressions and ideas that I just can't shake. This book is a perfect example. It started as an idea that I was not interested in at all, but I just couldn't escape it.

Ideas light me up. I love ideas! Lots and lots of ideas. Execution of said ideas, not so much. I just love thinking of creative, out-of-the-box solutions. I believe that's why God speaks to me so often through ideas–because I love them and I spend quite a bit of time thinking about them.

Here's what I know: whatever lights you up, however God designed you, will probably be a way that he uses to speak to you. He's kind to us in that way. However, every idea or impression that I have has to be filtered through the truth of God's Word to know whether it was really God's leading or just my own thoughts. More on this later.

Circumstances

One of the most famous lines from *The Sound of Music*, spoken by the Reverend Mother to Maria as she's leaving the abbey is, "When the Lord closes a door, somewhere he opens a window."[2] As cliché as it sounds, the Lord does often lead us by our circumstances, opening doors of opportunity or closing them as he sees fit.

Even the apostle Paul was directed in this way on his missionary journeys. As he traveled through much of what is modern day Syria and Turkey, it says, "the Holy Spirit had prevented them from preaching the word in the province of Asia at that time. Then coming to the borders of Mysia, they headed north for the province of Bithynia, but again the Spirit of Jesus did not allow them to go there." (Acts 16:6-7)

It can be tempting to want to bust through closed doors or refuse to walk through open ones. The challenge, and the beauty, comes in accepting and recognizing open and closed doors for the gift that God is giving us and the subtle direction he's providing through them. When we can come to these doors, and instead of trying to break them down or pry them open, we can truly give thanks for God's direction, that's when we know we've reached a new level of trust and surrender.

People

Most of us can identify at least one person in our life who is further along in their spiritual journey and relationship with God than we are. Perhaps it's a pastor, parent, or grandparent. But the majority of us can identify that person who doesn't just give good advice; they give godly advice. God uses these people to help us decide if something that we're contemplating is a good idea or something we should let go.

Sometimes they're able to recognize areas of weakness in our lives and offer wise counsel and strategies to help. This is what happened with Moses and his father-in-law Jethro, the priest of Midian. In Exodus 18:13-26, we see Moses overwhelmed and exhausted by the needs of the Israelites. Jethro schools Moses in the art of delegation, he takes his father-in-law's advice, and everyone is better for it. We all need a few Jethros in our lives who have permission to speak into our lives and whose wise counsel we not only listen to, but also put into practice.

Prophecy

Prophecy is one of those biblical terms that can make us feel like we need a degree in theology to even think about it. What exactly is prophecy and do you have to be some sort of super Christian to understand it? In the simplest possible terms prophecy is God using a human being to deliver a message. Sometimes the message is corrective (i.e. many of the Old Testament prophets) and other times it's meant to encourage and direct. The most important thing to remember about prophets and prophecy is to test their message against the Word of God and allow him to either confirm or refute their message through the filters that we'll talk about in the next section.

The Bible

If you're wondering what God's voice sounds like, in my experience, it usually sounds an awful lot like the Bible. Often when I'm praying and asking God something, he brings to mind a passage of Scripture. Or as I'm reading, something jumps out at me. But sadly, he can't bring his Word to mind if it's not in our mind. We need to read our Bibles in order to discern if the voice we're hearing is God or something else.

And if you feel like you never hear from God, at the risk of sounding blunt, when was the last time you read his Word? I can complain all day long that I never hear from my daughter, all the while she's been calling me every day, and I just refused to pick up the phone or was too busy to answer. That's what it's like to complain about never hearing God's voice without reading your Bible.

Any Other Way He Wants

We serve a creative God. He can speak to us through a billboard, a sentence in a book, a post on Instagram, a donkey (Num. 22:21-34) or any other way he wants. Our job is just to stay open and receptive and to recognize and respond when it's truly him speaking to us.

The Filters

Now that we've looked at some of the ways God can speak to us, we need to take it one step further, because not every idea, dream, or circumstance is from God. Fortunately, there are some filters we can use to help us decide if something is from the Lord.

Author Andrew LePeau talks about this idea of hearing from God and shares some practical tips about how a friend of his discerns the voice of God.

> "How does he make sure this isn't his unconscious talking or 'an undigested bit of beef,' as Scrooge thought Marley's ghost might be? Steve tests it against the Scriptures, the tradition of the church, reason, and the counsel of friends. If it is consistent with those, he moves forward. If not, he waits and doesn't make a decision. He continues his process of discernment, prayer, and listening."[3]

Without a doubt, one of the most reliable and trustworthy ways to hear from God is through his Word. It's a filter that won't distort or lead you astray. Psalm 119:105 says, "Your Word is a lamp to guide my feet and a light to guide my path." If something seems cloudy or unclear, we can hold it up to the light of God's Word and he will illuminate it.

God never speaks in contradiction to his Word–the Bible. Ever. If you're wondering if something is from God, you can very quickly discern one way or another by checking with the Bible. If it goes against anything in there, I can guarantee you with one hundred percent certainty it was not from God. This means we need to read the Bible. (Did

I mention we need to read our Bibles?) Let it saturate our hearts and minds. It's so much harder to tell if we heard from God if we don't know what his Word says.

Here are a few more questions to ask yourself as you seek to gain clarity about whether an idea or word is from the Lord:

- Does this bring God glory?
- Is it consistent with his character?
- Is this a verifiable way God has spoken to and guided me (or other believers) in the past?
- Have I talked to a godly friend about it? Are they in support of it?

If the answer is no, especially to the first two, it's probably not from God.

Now that we've talked about some ways to figure out if God is speaking to us, this brings us to the conundrum of what to do after we've heard his voice. As we've already discussed, the purpose of God speaking to us is to guide, correct, and encourage. To make us more like him. But that often requires that we step out and respond in obedience to what he says.

What if I Get It Wrong?

The final step in this process of hearing from God is our response. This can be the scariest part of all. Oh yes, listening can be hard, but taking action after we feel like God speaks takes things to a whole different level.

What if I heard God wrong? Who hasn't been paralyzed by this question? Especially when it comes to something as intangible as stepping out in faith in response to God's leading. (If you haven't struggled with this question, I'd like to read your book, because us mere mortals over here can learn from your self-confidence and wisdom.) Fear is a four letter word for a reason. It curses us with indecision and the inability to move forward. The enemy uses it to keep us stuck in a cycle of questioning God and questioning our ability to hear from him, ultimately causing us to miss out on what God is doing. Stuck inside our own heads, we never take the first step in the direction of obedience, no matter how timid it may be.

Let's pause here and admit, we're not always going to get it right. We are human. None of us think the way God thinks, or acts perfectly all the time. Sometimes we *will* get it wrong. This is where we get to remind ourselves this is a process. We're in process. So often we want everything to be simple. Straightforward. No ambiguity or mystery. No chance to get it wrong. But God invites us to more. He desires for us to use the wisdom he gives, the people he's placed around us, and his Word to guide us.

I don't typically like things with a process; I prefer to skip ahead to the finished product. I don't like IKEA furniture because I have to put it together. I just want to buy something pre-assembled, thankyouverymuch. But we learn things in the process, and the next time we face a similar issue or problem it's easier; we have tools in our tool belts at the ready. The same is true as we go through the process of learning to listen to God. As we tune our ears to him, a beautiful thing starts to happen. We find ourselves wanting to listen even more. What once felt frustrating and confusing, feels freeing and comforting as he whispers direction, purpose, and clarity over our lives.

Think about parents watching their child take his or her first steps. They're cheering, they're wildly excited watching them take those wobbly, imperfect steps. Good parents don't get angry or write their child off when they fall down. They help them up and smile as they watch them try again. In the same way, God cheers for us as we take steps of obedience and faith in response to his voice, even if they're wobbly and imperfect.

I don't know about you, but I'd rather go out knowing I took risks and stepped out in faith in response to something I believed God was speaking to me rather than sitting around doing nothing. We can trust that God will make it clear if we're headed in the wrong direction. (Return to our discussion of open and closed doors for proof.) If God has asked you to do it, he'll be in it. In many ways, stepping out and acting on what God has spoken should be the most exciting part of listening to his voice. You get to partner with what God wants to do, and in my experience it's usually spectacular.

So here I sit, almost four years later, asking the same question I asked at the beginning of this chapter. Did I hear God wrong that December day? In the grand scheme of things I realize that four years isn't really that long, but as I wrestle with that question I keep coming back to one thing. I've been serving God long enough to know that I often can't understand him in the moment. It's only as I'm looking back that I can see how perfectly he answered every time and how exquisite his timing really is. So for now, I trust and I wait. (See chapter six if you need to revisit this idea of waiting well.) And as I do, God keeps filling me with what Paul described in Philippians 2:24 as "confidence from the Lord." That's what I pray for each time I listen for the Lord's direction, and he's been so faithful and kind to give it.

Father, I want to hear your voice speaking to me. Help me grow in the skill of listening to you. Whether it's through open or closed doors, people you've put in my life, or the trustworthy words of the Bible, make me sensitive to your leading and help me step out in obedience and confidence when you speak to me.
Amen.

Breakthrough Exercises

1. Look at the list of ways that God speaks to us. It's been my experience that he often speaks to me in the same ways over and over, most commonly through ideas and the Bible. Did a particular method through which God speaks stick out to you? Does that tell you anything about yourself? About God?

2. How can you pay more attention to God's voice? Make a list of at least three ways.

3. Chances are we all have some things that God has invited us to do that we haven't yet taken action on. Pick one thing and take a step of obedience today, and pray that God will continue to guide you as you do.

Hang-up #7: Should I Even Be Asking God for This?
Overcoming Independence

CHAPTER NINE

I'll Do it Myself

"Some people think God does not like to be troubled with our constant coming and asking. The way to trouble God is to not come at all."

– D.L. MOODY

"God helps those who help themselves."[1] This is a phrase often said with a twinkle in the eye, and taken as gospel by most everyone I know (even though it's nowhere to be found in Scripture). It's a phrase I've lived my life by, to be sure. The independent spirit and I began our love affair the moment that, as a stubborn three-year-old, I uttered my favorite words: "I do it myself!" Perhaps it's been ingrained in me since childhood because I grew up in the US, a nation that prizes independence above almost everything else. We break out the fireworks and shiny brass instruments to celebrate it each July. We reward and applaud the self-made man (or woman). Without argument, it's the ideal we strive for.

As Americans we take pride in our bootstraps theology–if you work hard enough and long enough, you can achieve anything you set your mind to. Our currency boasts "In God We Trust," but that's not really true. We trust in ingenuity, lucky breaks, money, and anything else we can earn with enough hard work and persistence.

From the moment we enter the world, each of us is working our way towards independence. We're applauded for almost every step of autonomy we take throughout our lives. If you're a parent, you cheered when your child was potty-trained. (And you saved a ton of money on diapers too–bonus!) And if you're like me you couldn't wait until your sixteenth birthday so you could hop into your car and drive away to experience the thrill of the open road and a little bit of life on your own terms.

Growing up in a culture that prizes the independent spirit above all else, it's easy for that same attitude to creep into our relationship with God. If we're not careful, our posture in prayer can quickly shift from reliance on God to self-reliance and self-help. When that happens, we either begin to believe we can't ask God to help us or we think we can handle everything ourselves. Most dangerous of all, we start to buy the lie that's how God *wants* it to be.

This particular hang-up is so dangerous because it weaves its way into our lives so subtly that sometimes we don't even realize it's there. Quietly whispering, "You don't need to pray about this. You can take care of it. Save your prayers for something more important." As if we need to bank our chips in order to cash them in for something big later on down the road. We begin to stuff our prayers away, choosing to tackle our problems ourselves, and before we know it, it's been a really long time since we talked to God at all. If we let the spirit of self-help run amok, the only time we'll talk with him is when we run into something truly terrifying and completely out of our control.

When we fully subscribe to the spirit of self-reliance, we stop praying completely. We don't ask for God's help, because we think we can (or should) handle it ourselves. In a sense, we're saying, "Hey, I've got this. I can do it better." I don't honestly believe I can do *anything* better than God, and yet . . . I live that way all the time.

It's tantalizing to buy into the self-help and self-improvement craze, especially when it comes to prayer. Believing we can control our own destiny is a seductive idea to be sure. If we can dream it, we can achieve it! Insert all the other motivational phrases that dotted the walls of your classrooms from elementary school through high school here. It's a sentiment that seems to promise we can earn God's favor and blessing by the amount of effort and work we put in, a type of work-harder-you-can-earn-it gospel, an appealing promise that we can control our outcomes (and God) by controlling our inputs. I'll admit this idea has subtly woven its way into the fabric of my life so deeply that it's taken me years to recognize it and begin to extricate it.

Weakness is a Gift

Have you ever thought of weakness as a good thing? I'd venture to say none of us want to be viewed as weak. It's not a quality we willingly choose. We want to be seen as capable, strong; we want to do things for others, not have them doing things for us. Need makes us vulnerable, dependent on others. I don't know about you, but that's an uncomfortable place for me to live.

Paul teaches us a lot about the perplexing paradoxical nature of the kingdom of God, including this idea of strength being found in weakness. In 2 Corinthians 12 he talks about a thorn in his flesh that God "gifts" to him in order to keep him humble. This is what he says about it, "Three different times I begged the Lord to take it away. Each time he said, *'My grace is all you need. My power works best in weakness.'* So now I am glad to boast about my weaknesses, *so that the power of Christ can work through me.* That's why I take pleasure in my weaknesses, and in the insults, hardships, persecutions, and troubles that I suffer for Christ. For when I am weak, then I am strong." (vs. 8-10, emphasis added)

Paul acknowledges that it's at his point of weakness that Christ's power shows up and works in and through him.

So he doesn't just tolerate his weakness, he revels in it. Why would he do that? The only reason I can think of is that he's learned a secret that runs so counter to our culture that it's hard to wrap our minds around it. He shares two important things with us in this verse about learning to rely on God instead of ourselves. One, as humans we're often tempted to try to steal God's glory. Resting in his strength reminds us it wasn't our brains or brawn that got us through–it was God's. And two, humility ushers in the power and presence of God. Weakness and deep dependence on God is the path to supernatural strength.

I want the power of God unleashed in and on my life, but I frequently fight against the way he says I'll see it. Weakness. *Blech.* Humility. *Double blech.* I want to grab ahold of those good ole bootstraps we talked about earlier, pull myself up, and make things happen. However, Gretchen Saffles reminds us in *The Well-Watered Woman*, ". . . absolutely anything in this life that leads you to depend on the strength and sufficiency of Christ is a gift."[2] We don't often think of humility as a gift. Yet it was one of the most remarkable qualities of our Savior. He chose the ultimate path of humility, laying aside his status as God and taking on flesh–– *which he created.* Submitting to all the limitations, frailties, and nuisances that a human body endures so that he could rescue us from the consequences of our sin. What an incredible victory his weakness won!

In the same way, in the upside-down kingdom of God we die in order to live, we are great when we are least, and we seek to serve not be served. As we do these things we begin to see God show up in supernatural ways around us. Living this way requires us to see things a little (or a lot) differently though. I'd like to invite you right now to think of the most frustrating and confounding problem you're facing today. The issue you'd really like God to miraculously remove from your life. Perhaps it's really a gift? Meant to cause you to lean into Christ and then sit back in wonder as you watch his power made perfect in your weakness.

You may or may not know this about me, but I have a dream of being a traditionally published author. I self-published a book which I'm very proud of, *Holy Doubt,* but I've always wanted to hold a book in my hand with my name on the cover and the name of a big publisher on the spine. However, I don't have the connections or the platform to make this dream a reality. While there are things I can do to try and move the needle towards this goal (and believe me, I've done them!), the fact remains that it will take an act of God to see that dream realized. Writing and publishing forces me to acknowledge that I'm completely and utterly dependent on God. I've tried everything I can think of in my own power, and it hasn't worked.

Very frequently I've wondered why God asks me to continue doing something that is so clearly outside of my skill, ability, and networking capabilities. But I'm learning to see every frustration and failure as a gift, because every time I come to the keyboard or launch a new book I have to ask for his help. I have to acknowledge that I need him. And that's a gift worth more than all the publishers in the world knocking on my door.

After years spent riding the struggle bus, making frequent stops at Do-It-Yourself Town and Roll-Up-Your-

Shirtsleeves Station, only to be disappointed and disillusioned when my hard work never amounted to much, I finally discovered the key to seeing God show up and show off. When I blurted out, "God, I have no idea what to do, or how to make this happen. I need you to show me." I think he replied, "Finally, now I can do something here!"

But it wasn't easy to see that my old strategies and plans were futile. For years I thought if I could just find the right marketing strategy, or reach ten thousand followers on social media, the publishers would finally sit up and pay attention. But here's a sad bit of reality: I'm left with what I can accomplish in my own strength and human ability if I don't pray and invite God to help me. Self-help and self-reliance were the companions that convinced me for years that if I just tried a little bit harder, or studied the latest book on the subject, I'd finally see a breakthrough, but ultimately self-help and self-reliance failed me because (wait for it . . .):

I'm not all-powerful.

I'm not all-knowing.

Stunning, I know. This shouldn't come as a surprise. But when we fall for the intoxicating siren song of independence, we begin to live as though we think we're omniscient and omnipotent. Suddenly, the weight of every diagnosis or broken relationship rests solely upon us. We dive in trying to Google our way to a solution, and it's exhausting. And heavy. As followers of Jesus, we know someone who is all-powerful and all-knowing, and he offers us his help freely and without condition. All we have to do is ask. But we often spend our days pushing his hands away and stubbornly saying, "I'll do it myself!"

Recognize the Signs

Hopefully by now you're convinced that while independence is not all bad, it can have some devastating consequences in your relationship with God. But how do you know if you suffer from the do-it-yourself disease, the independence infection? Can you self-diagnose? Fortunately there are a couple of simple ways to uncover these subtle saboteurs before they wreck everything. Ironically, or perhaps by design, we can't identify and eliminate this mindset on our own though.

I always hated group projects as a teenager. Whenever the teacher assigned one, I groaned because every group had a slacker: the guy (Sorry! It was usually a guy!) who didn't do anything to contribute, but was more than happy to take the good grade the other group members earned. But the real reason I hated it was because it always took so much longer to get anything done when you worked with a group. If I did it myself it would be finished so much quicker! An old African proverb states, "If you want to go fast go alone, if you want to go far, go together."[3] No thanks! I want to go fast *and* far, thankyouverymuch. For years, I convinced myself that being a lone wolf was the way to go; I didn't need anybody. Strangely, I even allowed that mindset to apply to God.

In her book, *None Like Him,* author Jen Wilkin gives us a helpful, but searing, mirror by which we can examine whether we're attempting to live this life in our own strength and sufficiency.

They are:

Prayerlessness

Forgetfulness

Anger in trial[4]

One of the first, and most obvious, warning signs that we suffer from the spirit of self-help is choosing our solutions to issues and problems before we ever ask for God's help. I'm going to go out on a limb here and say if you struggle to pray (which is probably why you're reading this book) when you're confronted with a problem, your first inclination is not prayer. I can say this with certainty, because this is an area where I struggle. When you have a problem, maybe your first stop for direction and advice is Google or social media or your mom. There's no judgment here! As I've already confessed, I'm a recovering Christian self-help case. And I'm not saying you can't ever go to those sources. But is your first reaction to cry out to God?

My hand is up, ready to admit, I don't go to him first. I'm embarrassed to say, sometimes I don't go to him at all. This is an area I'm still working on, but God has so kindly exposed it, and he's helping me change because I'm learning more and more that the real work, the work that matters and truly makes a difference is the work of prayer. Learning to rely more and more on Jesus. This is the path that allows me to lay self-help down for good, trading it instead for God's help.

A Better Way

Not too long ago, we had the great joy of spending a few hours with my counselor, Jeannie, who walked us through a very dark season when we were missionaries. When she messaged us to say she would be in our area, instead of where she usually resides halfway around the world, we were thrilled and surprised. Living in a small town in northeast Iowa, not too many people just happen to be in the area.

No one can remember the context for this comment, but at one point in the evening, Jeannie looked at Jonathan and said with a chuckle, "You're very needy, aren't you?" She was only half-joking and he responded with an emphatic, "Yes I am." It's a joke we've adopted and made part of our family vernacular because he's decided to embrace it.

What would it look like if we too embraced our neediness? Not begrudgingly, but with enthusiasm? God designed us to be needy people. What if we leaned into that and accepted it as the gift he intended? What if we received his invitation to lay down the weight of trying to fix every problem or carry every burden with joy instead of reticence? What if, when we face a problem, God was our first thought instead of an afterthought? What if, like Paul, we could learn to revel in our weaknesses? How would that change our prayers? How would it change our lives?

This verse, penned by King David, the one dubbed "a man after God's own heart," says:

"How great is the goodness
You have stored up for those who fear you.
You lavish it on those who come to you
for protection."
Psalm 31:19 (emphasis added)

What's the opposite of trying to do everything for ourselves? Admitting our neediness. As David says, God's goodness is "lavished" on us when we come to him. It's an incredible trade really, trading self-help and self-reliance for God's help. We bring him the exhausting, heavy things we were never meant to carry and he gives us his goodness, peace, and provision.

*God, I'm sorry for all of the times I've chosen to cut
you out of the equation and chosen my own ideas
and solutions to the problems I'm facing.
Forgive me for preferring self-help to your help.
Make me more aware of my tendency to do this and
help me do it less and less. I want you to be my first
thought instead of an afterthought. Thank you for
wanting to help me and not being bothered when
I need you. Help me embrace my neediness,
especially my need for you.
Amen.*

Breakthrough Exercises

1. For one week, ask for God's help with something every day until it's a reflex and you don't cringe when you do it. Practice putting your issue or request into God's hands first, before you take it into your own hands.

2. Spend some time repenting for any spirit of independence that's caused you to rely more on yourself (or Google or social media, etc.) than on God. Ask him to help you move forward with a deep knowledge that weakness is a gift–one you don't want to return.

3. For one day (or even one hour), pray about everything you think about. It doesn't have to be a long prayer. Just a short shout-out. I believe this exercise reveals all the things we choose to carry ourselves without actually praying about them. I've been guilty of believing that thinking about something is the same as praying about it, but they're two very different things. One invites God into the issue or problem, while the other leaves me trying to figure it out on my own.

PART TWO

The Hacks

CHAPTER TEN

On Snowflakes and Oak Trees

Unleash the Power of Your God-Given Design

"For we are God's masterpiece. He has created us anew in Christ Jesus, so we can do the good things he planned for us long ago."
– EPHESIANS 2:10

My youth pastor was a big, burly Cajun with a mop of black, curly hair and an outsized personality larger than the entire state of Louisiana. He was loud, bold, and very Pentecostal. (He also told the best Boudreau and Thibodeau jokes, but I digress.) His passion for God was unmatched and obvious. And honestly, inspirational. He had more influence on my love and desire for God than almost anyone I can point to in my past.

Following high school graduation, I worked at my church office. I remember hearing his voice carrying through several closed doors and booming over worship music as he prayed during the lunch hour. As a teenager, I remember trying to model my own style of prayer after him. Imitation is the sincerest form of flattery, after all. I tried shouting, stomping, and pacing when I prayed, but it just never seemed to fit. It felt like clomping around in my mom's high heels when I was a little girl. No matter how much I wanted them to fit, they were just clunky and awkward. But I convinced myself that was the way "good" Christians should pray.

Because I equated passionate prayer and love for God with loud shouting and furious pacing, I struggled under the weight of shame for years, believing that unless I was yelling, I wasn't doing it right. To be clear, I don't think my youth pastor ever meant to make any of us feel like we were inferior if we didn't shout our prayers; that was just who he was and how he expressed himself to God. But I started to believe that something was fundamentally wrong with me because I really didn't want to yell during prayer. I silently wondered, *Why doesn't my love for God make me want to shout?*

Fast forward a couple of decades and I realized one day that I don't like shouting. Period. If this seems like a funny revelation, you're right, it is. And yet it was as stunning to me as the day I realized I actually *do* like blue cheese. *If I don't like shouting in my regular, everyday life, why should I feel like shouting in prayer is an indicator of my love for God?*

If you've been around Christians and church for any amount of time you've likely picked up some beliefs about prayer. The proper way to do it, when to do it, etc. We've already talked about this some in the chapter about perfectionism, but maybe you've felt the pressure to conform to someone else's idea of what a good pray-er looks or sounds like (or maybe even your own ideas), and it all just feels wrong and false, like you're trying to be someone you're not.

Take a deep breath.

Maybe it feels wrong because you've been trying to fit into someone else's mold when God designed you to function in a completely different one. What if I told you you can stop the comparison cycle that leaves you feeling like a failure every time you pray and consider that maybe, just maybe, you were designed for a completely different approach to prayer?

Don't worry, I'm not about to launch into some heretical new revelation about prayer. I'm just going to propose some practical ways for you to embrace who God made *you* to be and introduce some ways that you can learn to leverage your unique, God-given design in your conversations with him. Sounds like a pretty elementary idea, right?

Many of us have spent our entire lives trying to squash ourselves into someone else's mold, believing that there's one "correct" way to pray. We've gotten stuck thinking prayer needs to look a certain way—when in fact, God is the author of creativity and the capital "O" original. It's believed there are over sixty thousand different species of trees in the world.[1] Sixty thousand! And that's just one small speck of

God's creative power on display. Don't get me started on all the plants and flowers.

At this point in the book I hate to break it to you, but there's no one-size-fits-all approach to prayer. There's no magic formula. Just as each of us are different and unique, our style of prayer can be a unique reflection of the way God designed us. While that may seem discouraging at first, it should actually be liberating. Perhaps prayer has been frustrating to you because you're trying to pattern yourself after someone else's design. Instead of wasting time feeling irritated that you don't pray like someone else, you can get busy discovering how God created you to communicate with him. That's what this chapter is going to help you do. Honestly, that's what the rest of this book is all about.

To think that God designed all of us so uniquely and then somehow expects us all to pray in exactly the same way like little robots seems ridiculous and insulting to the breadth of his creativity. We know that God has crafted each of us with unique quirks, traits, and designs, and that it all brings glory to him. Mountains, rivers, and flowers bring glory to God in specific and distinctive ways. Why should we be any different? The key to all of this, to unlocking and unleashing your prayers, is discovering how to tap into your unique prayer personality.

What's Your Type?

I love a good personality test. Myers-Briggs, StrengthsFinder, the Enneagram. I've taken them all trying to learn more about what makes me tick. There's no shortage of books and tests designed to help you discover all kinds of things about yourself, but I've never come across a personality test designed to help pinpoint my personality as it relates to prayer. After realizing that tapping into our unique personalities can help us better connect with God, I decided to create the prayer personality quiz. It was created to help identify your unique strengths and then break down how you can use them to connect with God on a deeper level when you pray. You can go to www.ericabarthalow.com/ and take the quiz now. After you discover your prayer personality type, come back for a discussion on some practical ways that you can capitalize on your unique strengths and personality traits in your prayer time.

As I've already acknowledged there can be so much room for individual expression within each of these, but I've broken the prayer personalities into four main types:

1. The Contemplative
2. The Free Spirit
3. The Planner
4. The Socialite

Read on to learn more about your type and how you can use it to enrich your conversations with God. My prayer is that you'll find practical tools you can adopt and adapt from each type, but the tips for your prayer personality type will probably resonate the deepest. Let's get started, shall we?

The Contemplative

If you're a Contemplative, you're the thoughtful, quiet type. The one who likes to sit back and soak it all in. At a party you might like to sit by yourself and people watch (because who has time for small talk, yuck!), or you might find one person that you can have a deeper conversation with, or you might be asking yourself why you came to the party in the first place.

Your gift for deep contemplation extends to most areas of your life, and you prefer to take your time and not rush through anything. Because of this, you're very perceptive and easily pick up on other people's moods and feelings. You are also usually quite in tune with your own feelings as well.

THINGS TO LOOK OUT FOR

Because you typically spend a lot of time inside your head thinking, you can easily veer toward anxiety and overthinking. Philippians 4:8 can make an excellent filter for your thoughts. When you're tempted to give in to anxiety and unproductive thought patterns, ask yourself:

- Is this true?
- Is this honorable?
- Is this right?
- Is this pure?
- Is this lovely?
- Is this admirable?
- Is this excellent?
- Is this worthy of praise?

If the answer is no, choose to consciously redirect your thoughts toward something that will let you answer yes (2 Cor. 10:5)!

HOW TO MAKE IT WORK FOR YOU

I'm a firm believer that if you struggle to do something (like praying), the best way to start is small. You don't need a million things to try, you just need one *simple* thing that will get you moving in the right direction, and everything seems to snowball from there.

For you, dear Contemplative, because you spend a lot of time in your thoughts, it can be good to pluck your thoughts out of the swirling chaos of your mind and turn them into concrete prayers by journaling. Otherwise, you can spend all your time thinking about praying and never get around to *actually* praying and bringing those issues to God.

Today, use your strength of deep thinking to present God with one thought. Just one. Choose the one that you just can't seem to shake, and write it down. Spill out every detail about that one issue or problem, don't hold anything back. And remember as you write that God is present and listening. After you've fully unpacked that one, singular thought, take a moment to quiet your mind and listen for his voice.

The Free Spirit

For the Free Spirit, variety is the spice of life. You prefer spontaneity to structure, and restrictions and routines are a real bummer. You're creative, inventive, and adaptive. Easily going with the flow, you enjoy trying new things and you're always up for adventure. For a Free Spirit, boredom is public enemy number one. You're always chasing that next fun or thrilling experience. For you, life is what you make it, and you aim to make it vibrant and rich.

THINGS TO LOOK OUT FOR

Because you dislike routines, it can be easy for prayer to slide right off of your radar and be forgotten for long periods of time. And if your prayer life has become boring, you may abandon the practice altogether which leaves you feeling guilty and defeated. But it doesn't have to be this way!

HOW TO MAKE IT WORK FOR YOU

Because you lose interest when prayer slips into a rote routine, the best way to avoid this is to create a new approach to prayer each day. But how exactly do you do that?

I'm glad you asked.

First, at the risk of stating the obvious, you'll need to set aside time to pray because if we don't make space for prayer it will never happen. But let that time and space be the only thing that remains constant and unchanging. The method is up for grabs.

Prayer is simply about connecting with God, and for too long I think we've defined it too narrowly. In the Old Testament we see examples of people building things as an act of worship and connection with God (i.e. the Tabernacle, Temple, and altars to name a few). As they did these things, their minds were focused on and praising God with each movement and task. You can benefit from following their example.

I love this quote from the old movie *Chariots of Fire* where the main character Eric Liddell says, "I believe God made me for a purpose . . . and he also made me fast. And when I run, I feel his pleasure."[2] As a Free Spirit, where do you feel God's pleasure resting on you? Is it when you run, like Liddell? Or perhaps it's when you play music, like Bach? Can you imagine telling Bach that music was not an acceptable way to connect with God? The key to using these things that God has gifted and created you to do in prayer is to focus your mind as you do them. If it's painting, you can thank God for your ability to bring beauty to the world through color.

You get the idea. Whether it's journaling, writing or playing a song, writing a poem, dancing, painting, reading the Bible or a book of prayers, or building something, the key is being intentional, focusing on God as you keep your body active and engaged.

Keep your prayer life fresh and engaging by switching it up; don't do the same thing two days in a row. Consider this permission to get creative; use your God-given personality to express your love and devotion to God in ways that you find engaging and exciting.

The Planner

Planners are some of my favorite kinds of people. As someone who regularly plans big events, but is *not* a planner, I appreciate having you on my team ever so much! You are the one with a plan for your plan. You want to know what you're having for supper . . . while you're eating breakfast. You're always thinking ahead. Your lists have lists. You are the person that people can count on! If you said you'll do it, it's as good as done. You're trustworthy and reliable, and absolutely nothing gets by you.

THINGS TO LOOK OUT FOR

You don't need me to tell you that it can really throw you off when your best laid plans go awry. Of this you are painfully aware. You struggle when things are unpredictable and you don't know what will happen next. However, sometimes the best moments with God happen when you least expect it and you can't plan for them. You can practice appreciating (or at the very least, surviving) these moments by taking a minute to breathe deeply and thanking God that he's in the midst of the chaos with you. This might sound trite, and it is if you just read it and don't put it into practice. But deep breathing and gratitude have both been proven to help relieve stress and change your outlook. Try it—it just might change your life the next time it feels like life is spiraling out of your control.

HOW TO MAKE IT WORK FOR YOU

One of the best ways to stay focused in prayer is to make a prayer list, but we've already established that of all the prayer personalities, you are the most likely to have that covered. We talked about this in the chapter on boredom, but I want to revisit it because it's so powerful. Don't let the fact that I just challenged you to make a list cause you to roll your eyes. Instead, lean in, and pull out your notepad and favorite pen. (I know you have one.)

Think of three (or more) huge prayer requests–if it seems impossible, it belongs on the list–and write them down. Maybe you'll write down the name of someone who seems like the least likely person to accept Jesus as their Savior. One of the things I'm currently praying for is a spiritual awakening and revival to spread through our local public school system. Talk about a big dream!

The Bible tells us that when we ask anything according to God's will that he hears and acts (1 John 5:14-15). If your requests fall into that category (salvation, God's presence and activity at work in the world, for his glory to be on display etc.), you can bet that he's all about it. So you get the joy of creating the list and bringing your requests to God and then waiting with expectation for him to show up. I don't know about you, but I'll show up for that all day, every day!

The Socialite

You are a rare bird. A unique creature. A social animal. In a world of introverts you are an exuberant and unapologetic extrovert, always the life of the party, *and* always ready for one! The phrase, "The more the merrier," could have been written by you—or about you. You have a magnetic and warm personality that draws people in, and a natural gift for making people feel welcome and at ease in your presence.

THINGS TO LOOK OUT FOR

Because you thrive on social interaction, your schedule can quickly get so full that it crowds out time with God. You might also struggle to be still and quiet and focus your mind during prayer because it tends to race in a million different directions. Fortunately, I have some great tips that can help you not only lean into your unique personality, but also make spending time with God that much more satisfying and rewarding.

HOW TO MAKE IT WORK FOR YOU

Your love for people and spending time with them can be both a gift and a curse. While it's lovely to spend time with people, we don't want it to come at the expense of spending time with God. But with the right approach and intentionality, your personality type really can infuse rich dimension into your prayer life. Here are two simple ways you can do just that:

1. **Create a Prayer Group.** Getting together with friends regularly (either monthly, every other week, or weekly) to pray for each other will keep you motivated and energized—and make prayer that much more exciting for you. For you, prayer + friends = a winning combination!
2. **Choose a Friend to Pray For & Text.** Another creative way to include friends in your prayer life is to choose

a friend per day (or a couple per week if every day is too much) to text asking them how you can pray for them—and then do it! If you're comfortable, write out your prayer for them in a text and send it back to them, or just text them a simple response saying you prayed for their request. It will bless both of you!

It can be tempting to compare our prayers and style of prayer with others, wishing we could be more like them. However, I hope that exploring your prayer personality has given you a new appreciation for the way God designed you and stirred your curiosity to investigate some fresh ways to connect with God. I pray you'll spend less time envying someone else's prayer life and more time relishing your newfound personal and unique connection with God.

God, thank you so much for crafting me with such creativity. Help me appreciate the uniqueness of your design and purpose for me, not wasting time feeling jealous about someone else's design. Teach me to be content with the way you created me and how to capitalize on it to connect with you more.
Amen.

Breakthrough Exercises

1. Put the suggestion for your particular prayer personality into practice for one week and see how it affects your prayer life.

2. If you want to mix it up, try one of the suggestions for a different prayer personality and see if it helps you connect with God.

3. What have you learned about your unique personality that you can use to talk with God more? Read Ephesians 3:10 and 4:7-16. What do these passages indicate about God's creativity and the variety of gifts he gives?

CHAPTER ELEVEN

Sixty-Six Words

A Fresh Perspective on Prayer

"Therefore, you should pray like this . . ."
– Jesus (Matt. 6:9)

I don't want to overstate this, but this small, yet mighty, chapter may well be worth the price of the entire book. It's like Mother Teresa, short but powerful. Clear your calendar and don't stop now because what I'm about to share with you is the star on top of the Christmas tree or the sage in your Thanksgiving stuffing. It's the essential element without which everything else, especially your prayer life, stays pretty ordinary and ho-hum.

For years I imagined God had a log somewhere next to the Book of Life where he wrote down the requests and petitions of those who said "acceptable" prayers (of appropriate length and depth), and I was sure mine never made it on his list. Disqualifying my prayers before I even uttered them, I told myself, "Your prayers are too short. Too insignificant. God only takes long, eloquent prayers seriously." Shame over the elegant words I failed to say kept me from saying any words at all. Maybe you've felt this way too, had these same sad conversations with yourself? As a result, every prayer you intend to pray sticks in your throat like a dry clump of peanut butter.

I used to think I had to "get alone with God" and pray for a minimum of thirty minutes in order to be doing it "right." Somehow I convinced myself, even though I'm not a long-winded person, that I need to babble on and on in order for God to hear me, as if there's some magical word count that unlocks the favor of God. I don't think I'm alone in thinking that if I just say *all* the words then God will have to answer. Surely Jesus was kidding when he said, "When you pray, don't babble on and on as the Gentiles do. They think their prayers are answered merely by repeating their words again and again. Don't be like them, for your Father knows exactly what you need even before you ask him!" (Matthew 6:7-8)

In case you're worried, rest assured that the heart of this chapter isn't about taking the easy road out and saying the least amount of words possible when we pray. It's about shifting our thinking to believe that a few words can actually be an effective and powerful prayer. It's not about laziness; it's about releasing those of us who aren't big talkers from self-inflicted shame about the length of our prayers.

Perhaps we should have answered this sooner, but what exactly is prayer? Does it have required elements? A formula?

A prescribed length? It's high time we defined it, both what it is–and what it isn't. Because if Paul told us to pray continually (1 Thess. 5:17), I think we may be overcomplicating it.

Early in the book we talked about the perfect pray-er, and I asked you to define what that looks like to you. Now I'd like you to do the same for prayer. Whether you've ever taken the time to write it down, you probably have some subconscious ideas about what prayer is–and what it's not. When I did this exercise, I realized I envisioned God holding an invisible checklist of undefined requirements that he measured my prayers against. And I constantly felt like I never measured up.

One of the leading factors, and an unspoken reason, that many people struggle to pray is their own amorphous ideas of what constitutes a prayer. At best, it's a loosely defined term and at worst the nebulous shape of our own ideas keep us feeling like a failure because we can't reach a target we haven't defined. I debated whether this chapter belonged in the hang-ups section or the hacks section because this is clearly a hang-up. But what I discovered as I wrestled through this particular problem in my own prayer journey has become the most helpful hack I've found for releasing me to finally pray with unencumbered freedom.

Wouldn't it be nice to let go of anything we're holding on to that isn't in line with what God expects and actually know what he says prayer should be? Besides the Lord's Prayer, does God have anything else to say on the subject? I'm glad you asked because this is where things get really interesting.

Doing the Math

I'm not a fan of math. Numbers and I are not on good terms. (Do you see what I did there? If you're not impressed by dad jokes–told by moms–I apologize. But believe me when I say this: it's well worth the eye roll my son will give when he sees it. Small pleasures, my friend.) It's a thing. Just ask anyone in my immediate family. You do not want me dealing with your finances. Even simple addition can be a real problem. (I did it again! Ok, I'm done now.) On the upside, no one ever asks me to help them with their math homework. So no one was more surprised than me that I would utter the words "numbers" and "life-changing" in the same sentence.

One day, while reading my Bible, I noticed that some of the recorded prayers in the Old Testament are kind of short. That got me thinking, *I wonder how long some of the other prayers in the Bible are?* This curious question set me down a path that has brought more freedom to my prayers than I ever imagined possible.

As I started to dig into the prayers contained in the Bible, I began to see that a *multitude* of the prayers found within its pages are succinct and short. So many more than I thought. This made me even more curious. *Exactly how long were all the prayers in the Bible?* Trying to find every prayer and reference to prayer got a little tedious, so I, of course, turned to Google and that's when the full picture finally came into focus. Upon finding a website that listed all the recorded prayers in the Bible, I sat back and thought . . . *Oh.*

Seeing all of those prayers in one place, broken down in black and white was nothing short of glorious. I'd encourage you to visit the website[1] and see each recorded prayer in the Bible with your very own eyes. It just does something for your soul if this is an area that you've struggled with for any length of time.

In case you don't have time to look at it now, I'll summarize it for you. Please don't rush through this part; let the implications of each statistic and fact sink fully into your heart and begin the slow work of untangling you from the belief that you have to reach a prescribed word count in order for God to listen to your prayers.

Here are those beautiful, freedom-speaking stats from hope-faithprayer.com:

- The Bible contains over two hundred recorded prayers (and a bunch more references to praying and instructions on praying) ranging from just two words (Jesus in Mark 7:34) to 1,205 (Israel confessing their sin–and we know that list be long).[1]

- The next longest prayer, coming in at 1,050 words, was Solomon's prayer of dedication for the Temple.

- *About 60 percent of all the recorded prayers in the Bible are* **less than two hundred words.**

Of the 222 recorded prayers:

- 110 of them (almost half!) were less than a hundred words

- 22 prayers were between a hundred and two hundred words
- 46 prayers were twenty words or less
- 20 prayers were ten words or less
- more than you'd guess (even one from Jesus) were in the single digits

My husband likes to tell me (and anyone else that will listen) that feelings are not facts, and while I usually roll my eyes when he says it, he's right. For years I let my feelings convince me that "biblical" prayers were long. The data told a different story. Stunned, I realized I had let some untrue assumptions dictate my prayer life for way too long. If it seems like I'm overly fixated on the amount of words contained in the prayers of the Bible, it's because I was overly fixated on the length of my prayers for far too long. What I found on that website began the slow, but important, work of dismantling my theory that wordiness gets God's attention. But there were more revelations on the way.

Teach Us to Pray

Without a doubt, the ultimate example of prayer comes straight from the lips of Jesus in response to his disciples' request that he teach them to pray. I find it interesting that those who spent the most time with Jesus felt like they were out of their league when it came to prayer, or at the very least like they could do it better, so they asked Jesus to give them some instructions. It's reassuring for those of us who feel like we don't have it all figured out either. There's no shame in needing to be taught to pray, and Jesus's response to the disciples' request was what we commonly refer to as the Lord's Prayer.

There are several things we can learn from Jesus's prayer that I believe will be so helpful for us as we finally push past the barriers in our minds that tell us we need to pray long, sophisticated words in order for God to take notice. Or even the belief that if we don't have thirty minutes to devote to prayer that we shouldn't bother.

When I picture Jesus praying, I think of all-night sessions with great drops of blood being shed. I envision him praying for hours at a time with great fervor and zeal. This might be where my deep-seated belief in long prayers originated, because there are certainly some references to all-night prayer sessions. However, it's interesting to note that the recorded prayers of Jesus are relatively short. I started to wonder if there was a reason for this.

So often we get caught up in our own ideas of what prayer should look like and what it needs to include, but in Matthew 6 Jesus's instructions on prayer remind us to keep it simple and direct. If you were to sum up his entire earthly ministry, you could describe it the same. Simple (not necessarily easy) and direct. His approach to prayer was no different. The length of the entire prayer he taught the disciples was sixty-six words (depending on your translation). I don't know if you noticed, but that's not a lot of words.

That realization led me to another question. How long would it take the average person to speak sixty-six words? Turns out, not long. Not long at all. It's here that I did a little more research and discovered the final piece of the puzzle that completed the picture of total freedom for me in this area. I discovered, "Most people speak at an average speed of four to five syllables per second. Most words are two to three syllables long, [which means] that the average person speaks approximately 100-130 words per minute."[2]

This means that the prayer Jesus taught his disciples, and the prayer touted as the example to pattern our own prayers after, was probably less than a minute long. If we speak at a rate of 100-130 words per minute, the majority of prayers in the Bible are less than two minutes long. I'm going to say that again. Most of the prayers in the Bible would take less than two minutes to say, and yet I'd spent years feeling like my prayers, which were often that same length, were worthless and ineffective.

This means that the longest recorded prayer in the Bible (Israel's) was somewhere in the neighborhood of nine to twelve minutes long. Sit with that for a minute. That's the longest recorded prayer *in the entire Bible.* So how did I come up with this idea that I needed to wear my voice scratchy for my prayers to be "good" and acceptable to God? I hope you're capturing the magnitude of this truth. If you've spent any amount of time discouraged by your short prayers, I hope you're starting to see there's nothing wrong with short prayers. Many of them made it into the Bible! They were the norm, not the exception.

As it turns out there aren't too many examples in Scripture where God disparages anyone's prayers. Long, short, or otherwise. In fact, the only example I can think of is found in several Gospel accounts. Let's check it out and see what we can learn about the type of prayer that God doesn't like.

> "He [Jesus] also said in his teaching, 'Beware of the scribes, who want to go around in long robes and who want greetings in the marketplaces, the best seats in the synagogues, and the places of honor at banquets. They devour widows' houses *and say long prayers just for show.* These will receive harsher judgment.'"
> (Mark 12:38-40, emphasis added)

The Pharisees (scribes in the above mentioned verse) were a powerful religious sect during Jesus's day. They were considered the religious elite, devoting their lives to studying and applying the law of God. Sounds like a noble ambition. However, no one drew more ire or harsh words from Jesus than the Pharisees. Why would that be? They observed the law to the strictest letter. Shouldn't they be the most pleasing to God?

Not so much. As it turns out, they were the kings of overcomplication and hypocrisy, piling the law on top of their fellow Jews, but not actually following it themselves. God was not condemning the length of their prayers; he was addressing their hearts. Their prayers were designed to get the attention of people around them and make them think they were something special. I don't think God cares nearly as much about the length of our prayers as we do. Once again, we come back to this truth: it's not about the amount of words we pray; it's about the attitude in which we pray them.

A sincere two-word "thank you" spoken from the depths of a grateful heart means more to God than a thousand beautiful but empty words. This is the heart of what Jesus was addressing when he condemned the Pharisees's long, showy prayers. It wasn't that he disliked how long they prayed (good news if you're the long-winded type). He disliked that they did it for praise from the people watching and listening, not from a desire to draw close to God and be heard by him.

Bringing it Home

As the truth of everything we've talked about in this chapter began to sink into my heart and truly transform my thinking about what pleases God when it comes to prayer, I started to realize I haven't been as prayerless as I thought. For years, I've prayed short, in-the-moment prayers throughout the day. Realization dawned bright and hopeful because if I added all those little prayers up they would probably equal a significant amount of time talking to God. I'd convinced myself those little prayers didn't count because they didn't happen in one long lump. But no more condemnation! I'm finally starting to understand that a sincere couple of words offered in prayer can not only be effective, but received with joy and great love by my heavenly Father.

An added bonus to embracing this mindset and the practice of praying small, short prayers throughout the day is that it helps keep your heart and mind focused on God all day long! The power of our prayers lies not in mindless repetition, showstopping and attention-grabbing fancy words, or even in a sheer abundance of words, but in sincere and humble hearts. God will never despise or reject that type of heart, whether it's offering two words or ten thousand.

I'd like to leave you with this poem I stumbled upon entitled "Praying" by Mary Oliver. I thought it was so simple and profound, and captured this idea so beautifully:

> It doesn't have to be
> the blue iris, it could be
> weeds in a vacant lot, or a few
> small stones; just
> pay attention, then patch
>
> a few words together and don't try
> to make them elaborate, this isn't
> a contest but the doorway
>
> into thanks, and a silence in which
> another voice may speak.[3]

*God, thank you for your Word and the prayers
that are written in it. Continue speaking freedom
over my heart as I lay down the shame and
condemnation I've felt over my short prayers.
Remind me that any time spent talking to
you is valuable and makes a difference.
Teach me to pray, simply and directly.
Amen.*

Breakthrough Exercises

1. The things we tell ourselves matters. If we want to see change take place, we have to change the narrative we tell ourselves. Try telling yourself a new narrative that your prayers don't have to be long to be good.

2. Visit hopefaithprayer.com and look at all of the recorded biblical prayers. It will change your life if you've ever felt guilty about the length of your prayers.

3. If you're still feeling insecure about your prayers, ask the Lord to teach you to pray, just like the disciples did.

CHAPTER TWELVE

Borrowed Words

Praying God's Word

"All Scripture is inspired by God and is useful to teach us what is true and to make us realize what is wrong in our lives. It corrects us when we are wrong and teaches us to do what is right."
– 2 TIMOTHY 3:16

My grandmother was an employee of Hallmark cards for decades. Even now, when I see that gold crown logo, a rush of emotion sweeps over me. Some of my fondest memories stem from those fleeting moments between Halloween and Thanksgiving before we plunged headlong into the holiday crush when she brought home a hand-selected Christmas ornament for me each year from the company store. I couldn't wait to see what she chose for me. (To my delight, it was usually a Peanuts character.) Every Christmas, when

I break out those ornaments and nestle each one snugly into an evergreen branch, I think of her, and the way Hallmark has been part of our family's celebrations and special occasions for years. One of the reasons greeting cards are so popular, and why we'll spend upwards of $6.99(!!) on what is essentially a fancy piece of paper, is because they perfectly express what's on our hearts. They have a way of capturing a silly sentiment or a lifetime of faithful love in just a few carefully crafted lines.

What if I told you there's a Hallmark for prayers? Unfortunately we can't go to a store and pull an aptly worded prayer from neat, orderly rows on display under fluorescent lighting, but there is somewhere we can go to find words that perfectly encapsulate every human thought, emotion, and experience. Words of comfort, celebration, sadness, and grief. For years, people have turned to the words of great writers and poets like Shakespeare, Austen, Lewis, and Frost to help accurately capture and express a romantic sentiment or even the beauty of golden leaves found in a "yellow wood."

Did you know we can borrow words from great writers of the past for our prayers too? We can lean into the wisdom and emotion found in the words of the early church leaders and fathers of the faith written centuries ago. Now that we've overcome the hang-up that we have to pray perfectly for God to hear us, we get to learn about perfect prayers. In other words, praying the Bible.

The Why Behind the How

The Bible is full of incredible promises. One of the benefits of praying Scripture, of speaking it out loud and agreeing with your heart, is it stirs excitement and expectation. When we align our hearts with what God has already said he wants to do, we know it's only a matter of time before we see it happen! But how can you know if you're praying in agreement with what God wants to do? How do we know if we can (or should) pray a passage of Scripture? Is there a process that we can use to determine if it's proper to present a certain request to God?

These are all good questions. Before we get to the answers, there's something we need to address.

My husband has the gift of woo. CliftonStrengths defines it as the enviable ability to "win others over."[1] In other words, he has the gift of convincing people to do things for him they wouldn't ordinarily do for someone else. It's like a magical power. Fortunately he uses his powers for good, not evil. Many a customer service rep has issued a refund or replaced an item long after the warranty expired for him. Let's just say they would never do that for me. But I'm not bitter. He can sweet talk the grouchiest clerk, and at the end of it all they both walk away with a smile on their faces. Sometimes it's maddening, but more often than not I love it! And they love him. (That part I actually understand quite well.)

At times I'm tempted to think that God works the same way. If I can just find the right words then, like Jonathan with those customer service reps, I'll be able to win God over and he'll do whatever I want. There were even a couple of Scriptures that seemed to support this idea and confused me for years. Maybe you've heard or read them too and wondered exactly what they meant and how they applied to your prayers.

> "This is the confidence we have before him [God]: if we ask anything according to his will, he hears us." (1 John 5:14 CSB)

> "In that day you will no longer ask me anything. Very truly I tell you, my Father will give you whatever you ask for in my name." (John 16:23 NLT)

These two passages always confounded me. They seemed to suggest that there's some type of formula that unlocks and unleashes God's answers to prayer, but it failed to tell us the formula. I'll be frank, I never found that I could ask whatever I wanted and God just did it. Some people claim that's their experience. But for me: Never. Happened. Were there some unwritten rules? Some covert caveats? What was I missing? Does anything actually mean *anything*? Does that verse in 1 John mean I can ask God for a new car? Shouldn't there be qualifications? Are there? These were the thoughts that swirled in my brain as I puzzled over these two passages.

Growing up, I heard a lot of discussions about the "will of God." There was talk about being "in the center of it," or "missing it." Either way, the will of God always seemed like such a difficult thing to get a grip on. There was a lot of low-grade anxiety around trying to figure it all out. And I think it's one of the reasons why I started to buy into this belief that there are "correct" words for prayers.

There's so much about God that is unexplainable, inexplicable, and unknowable. He'll never be reduced to a formula or manipulated like a genie in a bottle (thank goodness). Which leads us to the most important thing to remember: we don't pray Scripture because we believe we can somehow exploit or control God or find a formula that gets him to do whatever we want. I'm in no way implying that we can pick out a verse, pray it, and that God will do whatever it says. What I am saying is there is immense power in aligning our hearts and will with the things that God has already revealed he wants to do in his Word. The key to praying prayers that please God and release his power in your life lies in the ability to tell God, "Not my will, but *yours*, be done" (Luke 22:42). The more we practice this, the more we realize, this is the truly perfect prayer.

Sometimes Jesus spoke in riddles or parables; his meaning wasn't always clear and his disciples would often ask him to explain. As it turns out, it's not really that difficult to discover what God wants from us. As we read the Bible, it tells us exactly what types of things God desires and what he's pleased with. Here are just a few things that make his heart rejoice:

- Mercy
- Love

- Justice
- Obedience
- Faith

Words frequently fail me. That might seem like an odd statement since I've filled this book with thousands of them, but as I've already mentioned, when I open my mouth to say words out loud, it's like my brain misfires and I just can't think of a single thing to say. This is why I'm so grateful for the opportunity to pray Scripture.

Praying Scripture or reciting written prayers is not a new concept. The idea of using pre-written words to form the structure of our prayers has been part of liturgical traditions for hundreds of years. Books like *The Book of Common Prayer* have given voice to the deep groanings and great joys of people for centuries. However, I didn't grow up in a tradition that encouraged using written words as the basis for our prayers. We spoke from our hearts, and if that was difficult, well, you were in for a rough road.

The thrill I felt when I discovered that I could lean upon the words and experiences of those who've gone before me was liberating to say the least. There's nothing quite like stumbling upon a perfectly worded bit of prose that so succinctly and eloquently captures how you feel that it immediately becomes a beloved favorite. When an author somehow manages to wrap words around something you've been unable to articulate it feels like the sweetest gift. That's what praying Scripture has become for me–a beloved collection of words I can use when words elude me and my thoughts are jumbled or jangled.

When my words feel trite and tired, it's in these moments that I turn to the Bible, borrowing words that have been passed through the centuries by people of faith, and find fresh life to animate my conversations with God. There's a wealth of human experience and emotion there just waiting for us to tap into.

The Nitty Gritty

Once you've surrendered your heart to God's will, there are a few key principles that will allow you to turn almost any Scripture into a prayer. The first step is understanding what type of Scripture you're reading. Once that's determined, there are some simple questions we can ask and elements we can use to turn the passage into a prayer.

Each type of biblical writing carries its own unique characteristics and flair. As we look at each of them we can discover something to add to our repertoire that will transform our prayers into a beautiful symphony. There are five types of biblical writing we're going to discuss. They are: Historical narrative (yes, history can fuel your prayers quite nicely), Law, Poetry, Wisdom literature, and Propecy.[2]

Historical Narrative

This type of biblical writing is a historical account of events and happenings. It encapsulates the early history of the Israelites all the way through the early church. It might seem like this would be a difficult style to draw our prayers from, but we can learn so much from the actions of the people whose stories are recorded in these books. We can use these history lessons to ask God to help us avoid some of the mistakes we see recorded there or to cultivate some of the desirable character traits of biblical characters in us.

Law

The law does two very important things for us. It causes us to give thanks that Jesus came to fulfill its myriad requirements, thereby simplifying it for us, and it reminds us of the ways we fall short of God's holiness. It inspires awe, a healthy fear, and gratefulness to God for Jesus's sacrifice. Many people say that the law is irrelevant for us today since we are under the new covenant that Jesus ushered in with his death and resurrection. But Jesus didn't make the law obsolete, he fulfilled it (Matt. 5:17). Many parts of the law not only make good, common sense, but I would venture to say God still wants us to follow it. (Ahem, thou shalt not murder.)

Poetry

Biblical poetry is one of the greatest gifts contained in the pages of the Bible. Emotions can be notoriously fickle and difficult to express, but biblical poetry gives us the words to pour our feelings out to God, and the permission we sometimes need to feel all of our emotions. Biblical poetry provides some of the best passages to flip to when we need to put words to a particularly difficult experience, or even if we feel tricky emotions like anger, jealousy, or a need for vengeance.

Wisdom Literature

The Bible tells us that wisdom is to be prized, pursued, and honored. Biblical writers encourage us to ask God for it, and tell us that he's faithful to give it to all who ask (James 1:5). This type of literature is full of specific things we can ask God for as we pursue more wisdom in our lives.

Prophecy

This type of writing is meant to comfort or correct its readers. As such, we can use the words of prophetic literature to lead us either to rejoice over Jesus's coming victory or to repentance over any stubborn sins or willful disobedience we might be involved in.

As we work to identify what type of writing we're dealing with, it helps us use it correctly as we form our prayers. When we approach the Bible as the starting point for our prayers, we first need to have our heart and attitude right, and then we need to ask ourselves what type of biblical writing it is. From there we have the framework that will let us begin putting our prayers together.

Tying it All Together

As we discussed in the chapter on prayer personalities, there are as many types of prayer as there are people. For our purposes and the sake of simplicity I'm going to talk about four different kinds of prayer.

1. Praise

You can turn a passage of Scripture into a prayer of praise and adoration by thanking God for an aspect of his nature that was revealed in whatever passage you read. Whenever you read your Bible and you come across something that's particularly awesome or incredible, you can stop and thank God.

2. Question

Maybe a particular verse or passage was really confusing, and you're not sure what you were supposed to learn from it. There's no shame in asking God to help you understand it. You can turn that passage into a prayer by asking God what it means, what it reveals about him and/or his character, and how it might apply to your life.

3. Confession

Sometimes a particular passage brings conviction and shines a spotlight on sin and things in our life that aren't in alignment with God's Word. In these instances, we can use the words from the passage as a prayer for forgiveness and a way to express our desire to repent and turn from those things.

4. Request

Perhaps the passage talks about something you would like to ask God to do, or thoughts and attitudes you'd like him to cultivate in you. You can use the words of the passage to form a prayer asking God to do those things, or to shape your life so it more clearly reflects his Word.

If you'd like to see specific examples showing you how to transform each type of biblical writing into a prayer, you can find a free downloadable guide on my website. As we round out this chapter, let's look at an example from Psalm 3 to see how we can put this into practice. This passage is a great example of how to use borrowed words to express hard-to-say thoughts and feelings.

> "O Lord, I have so many enemies;
> so many are against me.
> So many are saying,
> 'God will never rescue him!'
>
> But you, O Lord, are a shield
> around me;
> You are my glory, the one who holds
> my head high.
> I cried out to the Lord,
> and he answered me from his holy
> mountain.
>
> I lay down and slept,
> yet I woke up in safety,
> for the Lord was watching over me.
> I am not afraid of ten thousand
> enemies
> who surround me on every side.
>
> Arise, O Lord!
> Rescue me, my God!
> Slap all my enemies in the face!
> Shatter the teeth of the wicked!

Victory comes from you, O Lord.
May you bless your people."

The Hebrew title for this Psalm is "A Psalm of David when he fled from Absalom, his son."[3] If you think you've got problems, if you think you've felt the sting of betrayal and treachery, David's got some words just for you. Words you can borrow to tell God exactly what you're feeling. The raw emotion captured by David's situation makes Psalm 3 a perfect example of a prayer to use when our emotions are feeling less than tidy. Not that we've all experienced the pain of our own children plotting against us (thank the Lord!), no doubt we've all felt the crushing weight of betrayal in some form or another. You can literally pray the exact words of this psalm to God, or you can offer your own remix.

For our prayer practice I'd like to offer a remix from Psalm 3. . . .

*Father, I'm overwhelmed by betrayal and
surrounded by people trying to hurt me.
They're even trying to convince me that you've
deserted me. But I know that you're my strength and
my defender and that you'll never abandon me.
My confidence is in you, confidence that lets
me sleep in peace. I pray for your justice and
vindication to prevail. Don't let them triumph over
me. Thank you Lord, for your faithfulness and love
even when I'm struggling and feel alone.
Amen.*

Breakthrough Exercises

1. If praying Scripture is something you'd like to try, but you're feeling a little overwhelmed, just visit my website www.ericabarthalow.com where I have a detailed guide showing you how to turn almost any passage into a prayer.

2. Practice starting your prayer time with the most powerful prayer you can pray: "Not my will, but yours be done." (Luke 22:42)

3. Flip to a random passage of Scripture and try to identify what type of writing it is and then form a prayer from the suggestions in this chapter.

CHAPTER THIRTEEN

Inspired Words

The Gift of the Holy Spirit

"The Holy Spirit isn't weird."
– ROBERT MORRIS

Picture this: you've spent the last three years of your life with Jesus in the flesh. You know the warm chocolate shade of his eyes, the way they crinkle when he laughs, recognize the timbre of his voice, and the familiar shuffle of his gait as his sandaled feet stir up dusty paths. You've seen his miracles up close and in color. Watched dead people raised, blind eyes opened, and hundreds set free from demons. You've not only heard his teachings, you've seen him live them out perfectly.

Imagine one day he looks at you and says with not one hint of sarcasm or humor, "I'm gonna go now. But, honestly, it's better for you that I do. Because after I go, someone even better is coming." (I'm pretty sure I would laugh. Or cry. I'm fairly confident I wouldn't know what to do! Someone better than Jesus? Is that a joke?) This is exactly what happened to the disciples at the end of Jesus's earthly ministry. Check it out in John 16:6-8 if you don't believe me.

Each time Jesus spoke to his disciples about the approaching end to his time with them he talked about a "helper" that would come in his absence. ". . . I will ask the Father, and he will give you another Advocate, who will never leave you."[1] If I had been in their shoes, I would have been completely bewildered. "What in the world is he talking about? Who is this helper?" I would probably argue, "How could he possibly be better than you, Jesus? That's just ridiculous!" The confusion had to be overwhelming.

As previously mentioned in other parts of this book, I grew up Pentecostal, and we tend to place a lot of emphasis on the work of the Holy Spirit. Yet, even growing up in that context, I often wondered if trading Jesus in the flesh for the Holy Spirit really was a good deal. I figured I must be missing something though, because if you think about it, that's a pretty strange thing for Jesus to say. Unless it's true.

Over two thousand years later, not much has changed. There's still quite a bit of confusion and anxiety around the person of the Holy Spirit. Who is he really? What does he do, exactly? Is he going to make me weird? I've met some "Spirit-filled" people and they are, well . . . weird.

You might already be getting nervous about the trajectory of this chapter, because talking about the Holy Spirit makes you a little uncomfortable. I completely understand. Even though Jesus said having the Holy Spirit in our lives is a great gift, we still have reservations. Jesus promised the Holy Spirit would be our helper and our advocate. I'm pretty sure all of us would agree those are good things, so why do we sometimes reject the Holy Spirit and his help? Why do we run away scared and hold him at arm's length? I'll sum it up in one word: weirdness. Let's be honest, he's gotten a pretty bad rep in some circles. It just wouldn't be right if we didn't address the elephant in the room. Or in my case, the chickens.

Weird

As a pre-teen some of my earliest camp memories involved crowding into an austere, dimly lit hall, nicknamed "The Tab" (cool church-kid lingo for "tabernacle") tucked among the rolling wheat fields of Kansas. Each year, as predictable as a teenager asking their parents for money, the speaker would give an altar call to receive the baptism of the Holy Spirit, and hundreds of students would pack the altars shoulder to shoulder, waiting expectantly for the Spirit of God to fall. Let's just say I've gone back and forth, at various points in my life, between wanting more of God and being scared that I'd get it. Never was that tension more poignant than at camp. Every other moment, I was torn between fervently praying for the Holy Spirit and worrying that if he filled me I would do something completely embarrassing and strange. I'll be honest, for most of my life I leaned more towards keeping him at a safe distance. I didn't want to be weird.

Since I grew up Pentecostal, it probably goes without saying that I've seen some pretty odd stuff masquerading in the name of Holy Spirit activity. I once witnessed an entire church full of people (not my church, just FYI) clucking like chickens under the supposed influence of the Holy Spirit. I remember thinking, *If that's what Holy Spirit activity looks like–count me out!* But as Robert Morris says in his excellent book about the person of the Holy Spirit, *The God I Never Knew*, those people were weird before they received the Holy Spirit. The Holy Spirit didn't make them weird (or cluck like chickens). They managed that all on their own.[2]

If you grew up in a faith tradition that didn't talk a lot about the Holy Spirit, or you're new to faith in general, some of this might seem a little foreign or even uncomfortable. So I'd like to begin our discussion about the Holy Spirit right here and acknowledge that yes, sometimes weird things are done in the name of the Holy Spirit. But that doesn't mean he's weird. And he won't make you weird. Unfortunately, Jesus doesn't get to perform quality control checks on all the people who call him their Savior. Just as there are weird people who don't follow Jesus, there are some weird people who do.

But the longer I follow Jesus, the more I trust him, and if he says the Holy Spirit is an incredible gift, I want to be open to everything he has for me. And spoiler alert: the Holy

Spirit really is as good (if not better) than Jesus promised. But we'll get there.

For now, I want to assure you there's no need to be afraid of the Holy Spirit. As someone who has spent a big chunk of her life feeling exactly that emotion about him, I can tell you with confidence there's nothing to fear. After witnessing some of the things I'd seen, I was worried that becoming Spirit-filled, allowing myself to be completely open to him, would make me super weird. But that hasn't been my experience at all.

I'll be the first to admit that sometimes God does things in unconventional, even strange, ways (I'm thinking specifically of the story in John 9:6 where Jesus spit in the mud and wiped it on a man's eyes to heal his blindness), but never weird. And he never forces anyone to cluck like a chicken! I'll say it, that is super weird. That was not a display of the Holy Spirit at work. It was a gathering of people who were no doubt hungry for and passionate about God but not at all educated about the Holy Spirit and his purpose in our lives.

One thing I do know, I undervalued and limited the work of the Holy Spirit in my life until my hunger outweighed my hesitancy that I would be perceived as weird. Choosing to let go of my fear and allowing the Holy Spirit complete access to my life is the best decision I've ever made. And I haven't looked back. By the way, I'm also no weirder than I was before. (My kids will tell you that I was definitely weird before.)

Now that I've (hopefully) put you at ease, and alleviated any fears that the Holy Spirit will turn you into a weirdo, let's see how his presence at work in your life can supercharge your prayer life. Because his help as it relates to our prayers is nothing short of incredible.

The Helper

My husband is an Enneagram Two–the Helper. (You're learning an awful lot about him in this book!) If you know anything about this particular Enneagram number, you know they have a compulsive need to help people, hence their moniker. Sometimes, even people who don't want to be helped. My husband suffers from this compulsion, or maybe more accurately I suffer from his compulsion. I kid, I kid (sort of). It's in his nature, and he just can't seem to escape it. Sometimes it backfires, but most of the time people love his helpful nature. He is quite loveable . . . and helpful.

Depending on your translation of the Bible, the Holy Spirit is described as a helper and/or an advocate. But what does that mean? How exactly does he help us?

As a teenager I spent many, many nights worried about "being a witness" for God. I stressed and fretted about what I would say, and more importantly how my friends would react to my witnessing. What can I say? Early 90s church culture was very focused on some rather aggressive evangelism tactics, and I'm not even remotely aggressive. If you've ever spent even a moment worrying about how to share Jesus with someone, or wondered how to talk with someone about your faith, then one of the roles of the Holy Spirit was tailor-made for you (and me).

In Luke 12, Jesus tells his followers that they will find themselves before "rulers and authorities" at some point in the future (talk about intimidating) and he tells them, "Don't worry about how to defend yourself or what to say, *for the Holy Spirit will teach you at that time what needs to be said."* (vs. 12, emphasis added)

This is great news for someone who frequently has no idea what to pray. Or what to say. Or who frequently says the wrong thing. Basically, it's better if I stick to writing, where I can edit until I get it right! I really should have recognized the gift that the Holy Spirit is a lot sooner. He teaches us what to say! As we have opportunities to testify about him, he guides our words so we speak the truth. I couldn't love that more. What a comfort to know that I don't need to stress and strain to try and put the perfect speech together. The Holy Spirit is my helper when I talk to people about God as well as when I talk to God. But I'm getting ahead of myself.

One essential requirement for a helper is that they be present. As Jesus pointed out to his disciples, he was no longer going to be with them in the flesh, and this is where the promise of the Holy Spirit gets really good.

For most of my life I thought that if I could just see Jesus with my eyes, drink a cup of tea with him, ask him my questions, and hear him answer in his out loud voice that I would be all set. All my problems would be solved. Maybe you've had the same fantasies?

As I've already confessed, I've spent large swaths of my life in what can only be described as jealousy over the way some people in the Bible spoke with God. I mean who wouldn't want to hear the audible voice of God give them direction, instruction, and correction? (Ok, it would probably be a little scary too, but so unmistakably clear.) I believed these biblical characters were walking around having conversations with God all the time. But that really wasn't the case. They would often go long stretches without hearing from him at all, and when they did finally hear from him, many times it was through a prophet. Moses was counted among the ranks of those who spoke with God most often, but he had to put up with a grumbling, complaining bunch of people and wander in the wilderness for years! No thanks.

As I wrestled with this question of whether it could possibly be better to have the Holy Spirit with us always, instead of Jesus in the flesh, I came upon a few important attributes of the Holy Spirit that I've taken for granted. Chief among these traits is his constant, abiding presence. We get the privilege of having the Holy Spirit with us all the time, in every moment. God with us.

Instead of feeling jealous of the way God showed up and spoke to people in the Old Testament, I was reminded that the thing humanity has longed for, intimacy and friendship with God, was ushered in by Jesus's sacrifice and then sealed with the sending of the Holy Spirit to dwell within us. The Holy Spirit, dwelling within us, was God's plan to be near and with humanity for all time. Not just for thirty-three short years. For always.

The Advocate

In our house, I'm the advocate. My kids swear that every plan or request has a better chance of getting a yes from their dad if I present their case first. I think they're really just buttering me up and saying, not so subtly, that I'm the soft one. The easy target. The one most likely to say yes without asking a thousand questions.

How does all this talk about the Holy Spirit as our helper and advocate relate to prayer? I'm glad you asked because this is actually my favorite part about the Holy Spirit. We don't use the word advocate a lot these days, but an advocate is one who "pleads the cause of another."[3] They're also described as a "champion, a spokesman, or someone who fights on your behalf."[3]

Who needs an advocate, you might be wondering. People who can't speak up for themselves, that's who. I've found myself needing an advocate more times than I'd like to share. Times when my heart was so broken that my mind couldn't put a single comprehensible or cohesive thought together. I didn't even know how to begin to approach God to ask for help. It's in these moments when the role of the Holy Spirit as my advocate is not only appreciated, it's essential.

Romans 8:26 tells us something that's almost too incredible to fully grasp:

> "And the Holy Spirit helps us in our weakness. For example, we don't know what God wants us to pray for. *But the Holy Spirit prays for us with groanings that cannot be expressed in words.* And the Father who knows all hearts knows what the Spirit is saying, for *the Spirit pleads for us believers in harmony with God's own will.*" (emphasis added)

Did you get that? The Third Person of the Trinity is pleading your cause, speaking up for you, making perfect petition before God on your behalf. The sheer extravagance and impossibility that God would do this for us is almost incomprehensible. When we have no words, when we don't know what we should pray for, when we're clueless, it's exactly those moments that the Holy Spirit prays for us.

He advocates for us.

He intercedes for us.

This is a miracle. The Holy Spirit prays for you when you don't know what to say. And if you're like me, he stays pretty busy. As I've studied the Holy Spirit and more importantly, experienced his power at work in my life, I've come to the conclusion that I've vastly underestimated how great of a gift the Holy Spirit really is. Perhaps you have too?

With the potential for so much oddity and peculiarity, why would I encourage you to lean into the Holy Spirit? Returning to Jesus's words, I'm clinging to the stubborn belief that he knew what he was talking about when he proclaimed the Holy Spirit to be a gift. Even in the midst of any trepidation that you may feel, I encourage you to try leaning on the strength and power that the Holy Spirit offers in all areas of our lives, but especially our prayers. When the Spirit is present anything is possible. Miracles are likely. And his power is available to you, in ever-increasing supply, all you have to do is ask.

Father, I want everything you have for me,
and I'm open to more of your Holy Spirit in my life.
Let your Spirit empower my prayers and advocate
for me before your throne. Help me not to be afraid
of the Holy Spirit, but to recognize him for the gift
that you promised he would be.
Amen.

Breakthrough Exercises

1. Have you ever had a strange encounter with someone who was "Spirit-filled"? How do you think that has influenced your view of the Holy Spirit? If you've kept him at arm's length, ask God to help your hunger outweigh your hesitancy.

2. Next time you don't know what to pray, ask the Holy Spirit to advocate for you.

3. Spend some time meditating on Romans 8:26, letting the significance of the truth contained in it increase your appreciation for the work and person of the Holy Spirit.

CHAPTER FOURTEEN

Where We Go From Here

Living it Out Today and All the Days After

"But I will reveal my name to my people, and they will come to know its power. Then at last they will recognize that I am the one who speaks to them."
– ISAIAH 52:6

Once upon a time I read a book about prayer, and from that day forward I magically wanted to pray every day. Wah, wah, wah. Nope. Not even close. We've made some great progress together, but I hate to break it to you. You're not going to be perfect (refer to hang-up #1 if you need a refresher), and you're not always going to want to pray. Or have time to pray. I'm not telling you anything you don't already know. That's why you bought this book in the first place. Before you throw it across the room and initiate a refund request, let's talk about progress. More specifically, your progress.

How do you keep this train rolling? What do you do when it's been a few days, or a month, since you last prayed, and you feel one of those old hang-ups start to creep back in, breathing its hot, stanky breath down your neck? Or when you really just don't want to pray?

A couple of years ago I joined an online pilates community called Lindywell. One of the well-loved catchphrases of the perky founder and leader, Robin Long, is "Grace over guilt."[1] She infuses it into every workout and email she sends. The message is simple, but profound, if you can capture it and weave it into the way you live your life: beating yourself up over perceived failures doesn't help, or make you want to come back after a break, but grace for a missed day here or there definitely will. She reminds us that our mat is always waiting for us when we return. Not in a harsh or judgmental way, but in a welcoming and inviting way.

Learning to live by this statement has released me from the trap of all-or-nothing thinking. Miss a day of pilates? Old me would berate myself and not show up again for a month or two. New me thinks, *I'll do better tomorrow!* It's an approach that completely changes my mindset about "failure." One missed workout is no longer viewed as a catastrophic blunder. Instead, I see it as an opportunity to begin again tomorrow.

Adopting this mindset in my prayer life has been a game-changer as well. It's not an excuse to skip praying and say, "Oh well, grace over guilt, baby! Grace over guilt!"

Instead, it's an opportunity to embrace another one of Robin's favorite sayings, "Do the things you need to do to feel the way you want to feel." It's inspiration and kindness over harshness and shame. I really want to pray. I know you do too. Don't you always feel better when you make the time to talk with God? There's something about time, any amount of time, spent focusing our attention on God that transforms our day. It's way better than pilates!

"Tomorrow is always fresh with no mistakes in it." This line is from one of my all-time favorite movies, *Anne of Green Gables,* and it's uttered by the unflappable title character, Anne Shirley. It's the perfect counterpoint to this statement, offered by her beloved teacher, Ms. Stacy, "Well, there's no mistakes in it yet."[2] A healthy balance between hopeful optimism and realistic honesty. When we can hold both of these together in each hand, we'll be prepared to move forward with a practice of prayer that's both life-giving and consistent.

These two statements sum up the most balanced way for us to protect the progress we've made together. We plan to spend time talking with God, maintaining hope and optimism that we'll show up each day to be in his presence. At the same time, we accept that we are human. We will miss a few days, life will get in the way, but that doesn't mean we are complete and utter failures as followers of Jesus. Can I get a hearty *amen* from anyone else who has finally been set free from the weight of that lie?

Remember our exercise from the distractions chapter? We shifted our thoughts to expect distractions, which gave us the freedom to accept them (maybe even use them) and move on. We can do the same with our expectations about the consistency of our prayer lives. There are going to be days when we don't pray for one reason or another. At that moment we have a choice. Are we going to allow it to loom larger in our minds than it needs to or are we going to remind ourselves that tomorrow is a new day?

Set your expectations now. You will have days where you don't pray, but you don't have to let that keep you from praying tomorrow. Don't let that ugly voice of condemnation stop you from coming back tomorrow without a hint of guilt or shame.

When Your "Want To" is Busted

I've done my best to be honest with you here on these pages, talking about things a lot of books would avoid or leave out. So we need to talk about what happens when you face a season where you really just don't want to pray. When your "want to" is busted. Because you will face this, even with all the best strategies and tools in the world. It's part of the human experience.

Right about now you might be expecting me to utter the old Nike slogan–"Just do it!"– aggressively encouraging you to just fight through it. But I don't think that's helpful.

The reasons we might not want to pray can be numerous and complex. Unconfessed sin, stress and exhaustion, or disappointment and brokenness, could all be contributing factors. Whatever the reason, there are a couple of things we can do to preserve our connection with God, even in the midst of a dark night of the soul.

If you find yourself in a season where your "want to" is busted and broken, the first thing I'd encourage you to do is spend a little time reflecting to see what might be at the root of it. When our desire to pray leaks out like air from a punctured tire, it's an indicator that something is wrong and we need to do some sleuthing to uncover the deeper reason for the change. Sometimes we don't want to talk with God because we're involved in sin, and we don't want to experience his conviction. Other times, unexpected heartbreak and questions just suck the words (and the breath) right out of your lungs.

While I *would* encourage you to keep praying, to push through, to "just do it" if you can, I would be remiss to overlook the fact that there are times when we just can't. If I'm being completely honest, there was a time when I didn't want to pray. And I didn't (except for the occasional angry outburst). And you know what? God still found a way to reach my heart.

If the reason you're not talking with God is because you're walking in unrepentant sin, confess it and get back into relationship with him. But if it's something deeper, more painful, it's okay to tell God that you don't want to pray and ask him to help you want to pray.

David was the master of telling God how he really felt. Even in the midst of all his raw, honest, and emotional prayers, he was still dubbed "a man after God's own heart." His example tells me that we're allowed to express our emotions to God, even if they're not pretty.

Some of the most shocking prayers you'll find in the Bible come from the lips and pen of David. You don't have to dig too deep into the Psalms to discover that he wasn't shy about asking God to destroy people, or to wipe the memory of them from the face of the earth. That's intense. He complained. He questioned. He cried out many times, "What in the world is going on? What are you doing, God?"

However, the one thing I notice about David, and the thing I want to pattern my life after, is that he always found a way, no matter how savage the circumstances, to remind himself of what he knew to be true about God. He never allowed his feelings to have the last word. (Though I'll admit this is very hard to do.) That's the kind of person I want to be too. It's the only way to claw your way out of despair or avoid dropping into that pit in the first place.

As you've spent time praying throughout these pages, finally letting go of some hang-ups that have tripped you up, I hope you've discovered a God that is so wildly good. I hope you've fallen in love with him all over again, and I pray that even in your darkest moments you can do as David did and remind yourself of all that you know to be true about God.

We've Only Just Begun

As we say goodbye, I want to leave you with this thought: there is so much more. This book is just the starting block of a lifetime of conversations with God that will grow deeper and more precious over the years. Think of this book, and all you did as you read along, like your foundation. You needed a solid start–the belief that you could actually do this thing, that you could actually pray–along with some practical tools to get you started. But God has richer treasures, deeper depths, and more of himself for you to experience. Keep going, keep building on this foundation, and I pray that with each passing day your love for prayer and desire for spending time with God only grows. I hope this book has increased your appetite for more of God. More prayer. More time spent in his presence. And finally convinced you that all of that and more is available and actually accessible to you. *You!*

I hope you haven't been overwhelmed by all of the strategies and tools I've offered here. If anything, I hope you feel empowered and assured that you *can* pray! Prayer is not reserved for the super-spiritual or those who dub themselves intercessors. Prayer, connection with God, is meant for all of us. I hope this book has given you an arsenal to fire back at the voice that pops up from time to time saying, "You're no good at prayer." I hope you can now confidently reply, "Yes, I am!"

As I write these final words to you, it's fall in northeast Iowa. Most of the trees have given up their leaves in preparation for the weight of winter. But as I went for a walk today, I was showered with an unexpected dusting of leafy confetti. Looking up, I realized not a tree around me still had leaves fluttering from their branches. It was as if the leaves were coming out of nowhere. I believe it was the Lord tossing nature's confetti to the wind, saying, "Congratulations! You did it!" Not only because tomorrow is my last day of writing, but because I've experienced breakthrough and victory in prayer right alongside you. At the very beginning I told you I was the girl to walk with you on this journey because I have the same struggles. Praying has never been easy for me. As I've written these words to you, God has used them to set me free from hang-ups I've held onto for years. I've never enjoyed praying more or felt less shame or guilt about it. My prayer is that you feel those same sentiments stirring in you as well. If so, I believe the confetti party was meant for you too! God is celebrating each step we take towards him, no matter how small.

As a mom of two young adults, I distinctly remember a moment with each kid where one day they were a child, and it seemed as though the very next day they were suddenly changed. Transformed into teenagers before my very eyes. Overnight. Of course it didn't really happen overnight. A subtle shift had been taking place for years, but I was too close to see it. It's strange how we don't notice small changes happening right in front of us until one day we wake up and ta-da! Suddenly we see it! Everything looks different somehow.

I've been praying for you as I write these words, praying that you've experienced big changes in your prayer life as you've read each page and performed each breakthrough exercise. But perhaps your changes have been subtle, more like the quiet, slow maturation of a kid into a teenager. Maybe you could use a little help seeing just how far you've come.

Think way back to the beginning of the book. In chapter two, we did a visualization exercise together that exposed any hidden thoughts we may have about what God thinks when we come to him for prayer. Let's return to that exercise again.

Close your eyes. Take a few deep breaths, in and out. Allow your mind to picture the throne room of God. At your feet, solid gold. God's throne sparkles and gleams as hundreds of jewels catch perpetual fractals of light that seem to be originating from God himself. The air is lightly scented with the rich scent of royalty and flowers. A light breeze gently ruffles your hair.

As your voice mingles with the cries of angels repeating, "Holy, holy, holy is the Lord God Almighty," what does God's face look like? As you approach him with a confident, "Hello, God, it's me again," what is his response? My prayer is that this time, as you picture his face, it breaks into a wide, welcoming smile, as his body tips forward in a posture that communicates you have his full attention. I pray a rush of excitement washes over you as you realize that he not only welcomes you, he can't wait to hear from you.

I'd like to leave you with one last prayer. . . .

Gracious Father, the one who loves us perfectly and treats our weaknesses and frailties with kindness, I pray for my friend as they go forward from here. I pray that you would speak total freedom over any areas that are still holding them back in their conversations with you, that they would lay down guilt and shame and walk forward in confidence that you hear their prayers. May their voice mingle with the voice of the angels as they declare your goodness and delight over their life. I pray this book is only the first chapter in what will be a long book of deep communion and communication with you that you're writing in their life.
Amen.

Acknowledgments

Some people compare writing and releasing a book to giving birth. Maybe because I'm fully in the throes of this phase of life, I think it's more like releasing your adult children into the world. There's fear and trepidation, wondering if you did enough, said enough, but ultimately, the job is done and the results are out of your hands. (If they ever really were in your hands to begin with, but that's a different book for another day.)

With that said, it takes so much more than an author to launch a book into the world. My heart is full of love and deep appreciation for the people who have had such a large part in this one. There's a long list of people who read this book while I wrote and helped me shape this message. A great big thank you to: Shelly, Carrie, Carolyn, Emily, Jonna, Tara, Angela A. and Angela G., and Melissa. This book is better for all of your input and feedback.

To the Sisterhood at Crosspoint Church, thanks for being my guinea pigs and letting me test this content on all of you! It's been a fun ride and I'm grateful to call you friends!

To my fantastic launch team—you all are the best! Thanks for helping me spread the word far and wide.

Mikaela-Your efforts to polish these words and make them shine is so appreciated. Thank you for lending your expertise and skill to this project.

Sarah-Thank you for your thoughtful and sensitive work making this book a beautiful experience for readers (and for me)! Working with you was a dream.

To my Tennessee family-especially Allie, who has a great love and interest in books and writers, thanks for cheering me on!

Mom and Daddy-Thanks for always encouraging me to write. Of all the things that have followed me into adulthood, the excitement you had for some of my writing in elementary school and high school is one of my greatest treasures. It meant more than you know. Love you!

Jacob and Juliana-One of the greatest joys, outside of your kids loving Jesus, is enjoying your grown kids' company. Thanks for being the most fun to be around. And thank you for reading my words and telling your friends about it-that's the best kind of publicity (and endorsement) a mom could ever dream of.

Jonathan-You've been my biggest fan throughout this whole writing thing. Time will tell if that was wise, but I seriously love you for it. Thank you for never giving up on me, and for putting up with my inability to meal plan and write at the same time (or do literally anything else and meal plan. Who are we kidding, my aversion to cooking probably doesn't have anything to do with writing.) You are patient, kind, and I don't deserve you. You are my favorite, forever.

Jesus–Thank you for constantly calling me to do things I don't want to do. Without you, I would be hopelessly lost and I'm forever grateful that you saved me and want to talk with me! *Soli Deo Gloria.*

Recommended Reading List

- *Pray Confidently and Consistently*–Valerie Woerner
- *With Christ in the School of Prayer*–Andrew Murray
- *Dangerous Prayers*–Craig Groeschel
- *How to Pray*–Pete Grieg
- *Praying Women*–Sheila Walsh
- *The God I Never Knew*–Robert Morris
- *Praying Like Monks, Living Like Fools*–Tyler Staton

Scan the QR code below to
find more resources to help you
flourish in your prayer life
at **ericabarthalow.com**

Free Downloads

Discussion Guide for *Praying is (not) Hard*
The 21-Day Prayer Challenge
A Simple, Step-by-Step Guide to Praying Scripture

Take the Prayer Personality Quiz

Connect with Erica on social media:

Instagram and Twitter: @EricaBarthalow
Facebook: ericaebarthalow
Pinterest: ericabarthalow

Does your faith in God feel fragile?

Do you wonder if there's any hope for the doubts you're experiencing?

You're not alone!

Through an honest exploration of questions like:

- Does God cause bad things to happen?
- Can he be trusted?
- Is God really good?

You'll discover how the path to a stronger, more resilient faith leads through doubt-not around it.

Get *Holy Doubt* today and find hope for the lonely road through doubt.

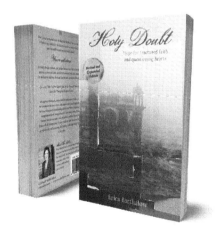

Love this book?

SHARE IT WITH A FRIEND!

3 ways you can share the love:

1. Post a review on your favorite booksellers site.
2. Get social. Share a picture and a few words about why you liked it on your favorite social media account.
3. Tell a friend about it! Or even better, buy them a copy.

Notes

CHAPTER 2

1   Luke 18:1-9
2   Philippians 4:6
3   Matthew 10:30
4   Psalm 56:8
5   Genesis 3:8

CHAPTER 3

1   Saffles, Gretchen. *The Well-Watered Woman*. Tyndale Momentum, 2021.
2   *International Churchill Society.* winstonchurchill.org/resources/quotes/page/3/ accessed 07 Jan. 2023.
3   Matt. 23:27-28
4   Abbott, Thomas Kingsmill. *A Critical and Exegetical Commentary on the Epistles to the Ephesians and Colossians.* Forgotten Books, 2016. Logos.
5   "The Art of Living in Wonder with Bob Goff." *Made for This*, 27 Feb. 2020, www.podcasts.apple.com/us/podcast/10-the-art-of-living-in-wonder-with-bob-goff/id1466667116?i=1000466833156e

CHAPTER 4

1 Murray, Andrew. *With Christ in the School of Prayer.* Aneko Press, 2018.

2   Cameron, Julia. *The Artist's Way.* TarcherPerigee, 2016.

3   Cameron, Julia. *The Artist's Way.* TarcherPerigee, 2016.

4   Trautmann, Jennifer. "Worn Paths." *Truly Magazine, Vol. 2 Issue 2, 2021.* Pursuit issue, pp. 22-23.

5   Batterson, Mark. *Win the Day.* Multnomah, 2020.

CHAPTER 5

1   Bradt, Steve. "Wandering Mind Not a Happy Mind." *The Harvard Gazette.* www.news.harvard.edu/gazette/story/2010/11/wandering-mind-not-a-happy-mind/ accessed 23 Nov. 2022.

2   "How to Hear God's Voice–Part 2." *Conversations with John and Lisa Bevere.* 27 Apr. 2021. www.podcasts.apple.com/us/podcast/how-to-hear-gods-voice-part-1/id218453800?i=1000516940420

3   Tharp, Twyla. *The Creative Habit.* Simon and Schuster, 2003.

4   "The Ecological Benefits of Fire." *National Geographic.* www.education.nationalgeographic.org/resource/ecological-benefits-fire accessed 10 Oct. 2022.

CHAPTER 6

1   Willard, Dallas. *The Divine Conspiracy.* HarperCollins, 2009.

2   TerKeurst, Lysa. *It's Not Supposed to Be This Way.* Thomas Nelson, 2018.

CHAPTER 7

1   Ephesians 6:10-13, 18 CEV

2   1 Peter 5:8

CHAPTER 8

1   "Discernment." *Wikipedia.* www.wikipedia.org/wiki/Discernment accessed 19 Oct. 2022.

2   *The Sound of Music.* Directed by Robert Wise, 20th Century Fox, 1965.

3   LePeau, Andrew. *Write Better.* IVP, 2019.

CHAPTER 9

1   "God Helps Those Who Help Themselves." *Wikipedia.* www.wikipedia.org/wiki/God_helps_those_who_help_themselves accessed 21 Oct. 2022.

2   Saffles, Gretchen. *The Well-Watered Woman.* Tyndale Momentum, 2021.

3   African proverb

4   Wilken, Jen. *None Like Him.* Crossway, 2016.

CHAPTER 10

1   "World is Home to 60,000 Tree Species." *BBC.* www.bbc.com/news/science-environment-39492977 accessed 21 Oct. 2022.

2   *Chariots of Fire.* Directed by Hugh Hudson, Allied Stars Ltd., 1981.

CHAPTER 11

1   "222 Prayers of the Bible." *Hope, faith, prayer.* www. hopefaithprayer.com/prayernew/222-prayers-of-the-bible/ accessed 4 Oct. 2022.

2   "How Fast Does the Average Person Speak?" *WordCounter.* www.wordcounter.net/ blog/2016/06/02/101702_how-fast-average-person-speaks.html accessed 4 Oct. 2022.

3   Oliver, Mary. *Devotions.* Penguin Press, 2017.

CHAPTER 12

1   "All About the Woo StrengthFinder Theme" *CliftonStrengths.* Gallup. www.gallup.com/clifton-strengths/en/252359/woo-theme.aspx accessed 25 Oct. 2022.

2   Wilkin, Jen. *Women of the Word.* Crossway, 2019.

3   Bratcher, Robert G., Reyburn, William David et al. *A Handbook on the Book of Psalms: Book One: Psalms 1-41.* United Bible Societies, 1993. Logos.

CHAPTER 13

1   John 14:16

2   Morris, Robert. *The God I Never Knew.* WaterBrook, 2011.

3   *Merriam-Webster Dictionary.* "Advocate." accessed 1 Nov. 2022.

CHAPTER 14

1   Long, Robin. *Lindywell.* www.lindywell.com/ accessed
     2 Nov. 2022.

2   *Anne of Green Gables.* Directed by Kevin Sullivan,
     Canadian Broadcasting Corporation, 1985.

Made in the USA
Monee, IL
15 September 2023

42808421R00139